€8·63

ONE-HOUR GARDEN

ONE-HOUR GARDEN

Joanna Smith

First published in Great Britain in 2002 by Hamlyn,
a division of Octopus Publishing Group Limited,

This edition published 2004 by Bounty Books,
a division of Octopus Publishing Group Ltd,
2-4 Heron Quays, London E14 4JP

ISBN 0 7537 0942 2

A CIP catalogue record for this book is available from the British
Library

Printed and bound in China

10 9 8 7 6 5 4 3 2 1

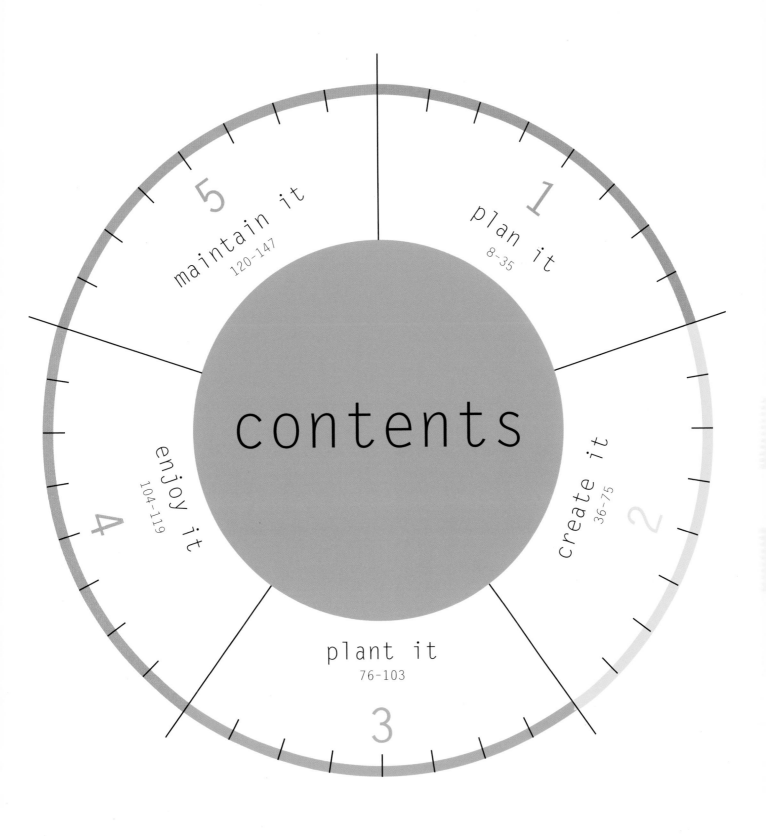

contents

introduction

Most of us take on far too much in our lives. We spend our time juggling work commitments with our families, friends, hobbies and home life to such an extent that we barely have time to keep the house looking good let alone to go outside and cut the grass from time to time. Yet most of us would like nothing better than to have a pleasant space outside, where we can sit and relax, soak up the sun, read a book, play games, enjoy long, leisurely lunches or invite friends for barbecues when the weather is fine.

Unless you are a keen gardener you are unlikely to want to spend any longer than is absolutely necessary on weeding the borders or pruning difficult plants, and even people who enjoy gardening would probably prefer not to have to spend hours edging the lawn or clipping the hedge. This book is full of ideas that will make it possible for you to have your cake and eat it: to have an attractive garden that does not take all your spare time to maintain. It shows how you can create a pleasant garden, suited to your needs and filled with the plants and features you want, that will take you less than an hour a week to keep looking tidy and inviting.

The book will guide you through the materials that can be used for surfaces, boundaries and other features and summarizes their pros and cons in a clear and helpful way. It also shows how to combine these features to create a stylish layout and offers plenty of ideas for making the garden look good as well as being simple to care for. The design of a garden plays a vital role in the amount of care it will need, and by choosing a simple layout, easy elements and a straightforward planting scheme you can have a stunning garden that stays that way – without a lot of hard work.

▲ Easy-care gardening is all about choosing plants that look after themselves, like these sempervivums.
◀ Dense planting is a good means of cutting down on the time spent working in the garden because the plants themselves prevent weeds becoming established.

A directory of low-maintenance plants takes the mystery out of planting. It contains a range of reliable, easy-to-find plants, highlighting their main features of interest and providing the information you really need to know about them: whether to put them in sun or shade, what type of soil they need and if and when to prune them. You need know nothing more about these plants than this to look after them. These same plants are used throughout the book to let you know which plants are best suited to the conditions that exist in your garden.

Finally, a self-organizer shows the main tasks that should be carried out throughout the year so that you can plan your gardening around your other interests and still have plenty of time to relax and enjoy the garden.

Throughout this book a system of symbols is used to indicate the degree of maintenance required by the various features, materials and garden layouts. The maintenance ranges from minimal or no care to some easy care:

••• minimal or no care   •• little care   • some easy care

Combining elements with different care requirements will allow you to design and construct a garden that is ideal for your needs and for the time you can spend on it. Although constructing some of these elements and altering your garden initially may be time consuming or expensive, these are the features that, in the long term, will allow you to become the owner of a one-hour garden.

▲ Choose an elegant design for a small garden with large architectural plants positioned for maximum effect.

plan it

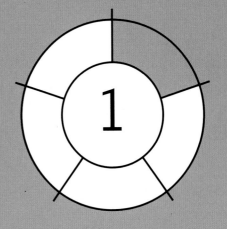

t is possible to have an attractive garden that takes just an hour a week or less to look after, but you have to be rigorous about the initial planning and limit the number of features and plants you include. You can easily create a stylish, easy-care, colourful space for outdoor living if you have an entirely paved courtyard garden, but if you are prepared to spend just a little time each week on looking after it you can do a lot to make it more enticing and interesting. You could perhaps do this by adding a shady pergola over an elegant dining area, clothing the walls with flowering climbers and adding a few flowering and foliage shrubs in containers or even a small water feature. In a more traditional garden for an hour's work a week you can, with a little planning, have time to care for a small lawn: with an electric mower it could take as little as twenty minutes to mow it once a week in summer.

Perhaps the biggest decision to be made when planning a garden is which type of surface or surfaces to use, and this is especially true of the easy-care garden. The proportion of hard surfaces, such as paving and gravel, to soft surfaces, such as lawns and borders, will make a big difference to the amount of work you will have to do. In the one-hour garden, you can never have too many no-maintenance hard surfaces. However, although large areas of handsome paving, interspersed with foliage plants, would be appropriate in a town garden, too much hard surface might look out of place in a rural setting. Always aim to tailor your space to its surroundings and consider using softer

'begin by simplifying the overall design of the garden and do away with any features or plants that don't earn their keep'

materials, such as gravel and slow-growing hedges, instead of hard elements, such as paving, fences and walls.

Organizing your garden is simply a matter of being strict with yourself and paring the features you include down to what you can maintain in the time you have available – although, of course, the garden need not look as if it was designed with that in mind. Begin by simplifying the overall design of the garden and do away with any features or plants that don't earn their keep. Rather as you do when you turn out your wardrobe, you need to ask yourself whether you really need that pond or whether the rock garden gives you enough pleasure to merit the time it takes to weed. It can be quite liberating to get rid of the features that have been making you feel guilty for so long because you haven't been able to devote as much time to them as you'd like.

You also have a future of far less gardening to look forward to. Although it may involve a fair amount of work to make the changes you need to transform your garden into an easy-care space, the time and effort spent now will mean many hours of time saved later – and you will get a much better-looking garden as a bonus.

◄ This garden may look stylish, but it is very easy to maintain. Paving and stone chips require very little attention and there are few plants to worry about.

▲ *(top)* In this courtyard area, very little maintenance is needed, except watering the herbs on the barbecue and plants in the containers and mowing the lawn.

▲ Honeysuckles, such as *Lonicera periclymenum* 'Graham Thomas', make good low-maintenance climbers as they need only be cut back once a year.

◄ Pots should be kept to an absolute minimum in any low-maintenance garden: in summer they will need watering daily.

why change?

We all want an attractive garden that we can enjoy, but we do not want to be a slave to it. There is no point in having a garden if we have to spend all our spare time weeding, digging and cutting back and have no time left for the simple pleasures of relaxing in the open air. If you feel that your garden is already making too many demands on your time or if you have just moved to a new house and want to have plenty of time to enjoy your new surroundings, begin by asking yourself the questions on the opposite page. If the answer to any of them is 'yes', now is time to do something about it and make some changes.

Many gardens contain too many fiddly features, often created by successive home-owners without any feeling for an overall design. Often a garden will have a number of small flowerbeds, a weedy vegetable patch, several fairly small areas of paving where different people have thought a patio should go and perhaps even a now-neglected pond, a rock garden and a few containers. All this adds up to a garden that is time-consuming and difficult to maintain because the different jobs are numerous and fiddly. There is much to be said for simplifying the design by minimizing the number of individual features, so that you cut down on the number of little jobs and improve the look of the garden at the same time.

Look at the features in your own garden in the light of the questions in the checklist and with the following list in mind. This will give you some idea of the types of job you can get done in an hour, assuming that you have been keeping on top of the work and that your garden is an average size. See the week-by-week organizer on pages 148–57 for more details of how this work can be spread throughout the year.

jobs to do in an hour

Think about the features that you want in your garden in terms of the time you can spare to look after them. Use this list of tasks that can be done in about an hour as a guide to deciding how long your ideal garden will take to maintain, and eliminate those features that, realistically, you will be unable to look after properly.

- Mow a small lawn and weed a small border
- Replant two or three containers with fresh plants
- Cut back six easy-care shrubs and dispose of the prunings
- Plant ten new plants
- Clear up fallen autumn leaves
- Rake over an area of gravel and top it up if necessary
- Give a slow-growing hedge its annual trim
- Look through some bulb catalogues and order a few bulbs for instant colour
- Take a trip to a garden centre and buy a few new plants
- Weed and top up the mulch on a medium-sized border
- Water, weed and feed all your containers

▲ Crocuses, like this 'Jeanne d'Arc', will pop up year after year with no effort on your part.

easy-care checklist

Would you rather be relaxing in the garden than working in it? Create an outdoor room like the one on pages 56–9 and look at 'Enjoy It', on pages 104–19, for some more ideas.

Is your garden a mishmash of features you don't have time to maintain or use?
Be brutal and simplify the design to suit your needs (see pages 16–17).

Are you starting from scratch with a new plot or are you adapting an existing garden?
See pages 40–51 for some quick ideas for transforming existing gardens.

Do you want some easy-care ideas that you can adapt to suit your own lifestyle?
Try some of the 'off-the-peg' designs on pages 52–75.

Do you want a garden you never have to work in?
Create a no-maintenance garden (see pages 40–41).

Do you want an easy-care garden with style?
Pick one of the off-the-peg designs on pages 52–75.

Is your patio uneven and ugly?
Lay a simple, stylish deck on top (see pages 46–7).

Do you resent having to mow the lawn every weekend in summer?
Choose another surface (see pages 30–35) or have a low-mow meadow lawn (see page 75).

Do you spend hours clipping the lawn edges?
Incorporate a mowing strip (see pages 132–3).

Do your plants look weak and weedy?
They may not be growing in the conditions that suit them (see pages 140–45).

Do your borders contain a profusion of plants that you don't know how to care for?
Transform them to a simple arrangement of easy, reliable plants (see pages 80–81 and 140–45).

Do you find there isn't enough time in your life to keep your borders free of weeds?
Make them into gravel gardens (see pages 64–7) or woodland borders (see pages 48–9).

Do you have a vegetable patch you can't maintain?
Get rid of it and grow a few choice vegetables in containers instead (see pages 94–9).

Do you want a safe garden for the children to play in?
Plan with them in mind (see pages 108–9).

Is your rock garden weedy and overgrown?
Either get rid of it altogether or build an easy-care raised bed for your rock plants instead (see pages 50–51).

Is your garden dull in winter?
Choose plants for colour in all seasons (pages 82–3).

Do you spend too long keeping your containers in tip-top condition?
Reduce the work by implementing some of the suggestions on pages 94–7.

Do you need some ideas for easy-care container schemes?
Follow the container recipes on pages 98–9.

Is your pond neglected or does it have broken, overgrown edges?
Plan it properly to make it easier to care for or install a simple pebble fountain.

Do you find yourself cutting the hedges several times a year?
Replace fast-growing hedges with more manageable hedging plants or opt for a no-care wall or fence instead (see pages 24–9).

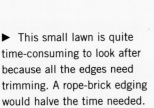

▶ This small lawn is quite time-consuming to look after because all the edges need trimming. A rope-brick edging would halve the time needed.

what have you got?

Presented with an established garden, many people will take the easy option and leave it as it is or tinker around the edges, ending up with a garden that is not a coherent whole and that does not entirely suit their lifestyle. Being bold and making the changes that will create the garden of your dreams and that you can manage comfortably given your other commitments is not difficult, but it means being realistic about what you can have and what you are prepared to do.

▲ Wicker and wood are the major themes in this garden. The bark mulch replaces a lawn, so only the plants themselves need care and attention.

time-consuming tasks

Understanding the fundamentals of easy-care gardening will be useful when you come to devise a plan to make your garden easier to maintain. Thinking about the most and the least time-consuming tasks in a garden is a good way to begin to work out which features to increase and which to reduce. Keeping on top of weeds as they continually pop up in bare soil beds and borders, for example, is one job few of us have time for, which means that this is one of the areas to consider as you develop your new plan. A little thought and a few simple measures will make those warm summer evenings a time to relax in the garden.

Look around your existing garden and make a note of how many of these time-consuming features you have:

- grass paths
- rock gardens
- bare ground
- several beds and borders
- rose gardens
- immaculate lawns
- summer bedding schemes
- vegetable plots
- herbaceous borders
- lawns with bare edges
- soft fruit
- vigorous fruit trees
- small, shady lawns
- island beds or other features in the lawn
- tall hedges
- lots of small containers
- hanging baskets

These are the features that you should be prepared to eliminate altogether from your new garden or, at the least, to minimize.

▲ This stunning array of foliage – in the form of rosemary, sage and phormiums – looks great all year and couldn't be easier to care for. Low maintenance need not be dull.

planning for change

Before you make any changes take a long, hard look at your existing garden and imagine how it could be. It's tempting to go outside and start work straight away, but there's a lot to be gained from a period of contemplation.

Don't forget, for example, that your garden will need to include space for utilities. Depending on the layout you may need to allow for a washing line, hardstanding for a car, access to the garage, an oil-storage tank, a tool shed, storage space for a lawnmower and even somewhere to keep the dustbins. Make sure that any new layout includes space for these items.

It's also important to decide exactly how much free time you will have before you can think about what type of garden you want. If you only have an hour a week, your garden needs to be strictly low maintenance, especially as bad weather may stop you from getting out every weekend. You will need to cover most of the garden with paving, with a few areas of easy-care shrubs or grasses and the remainder as groundcover. If you can spare a little more time, you could add a flowerbed or have a hedge instead of a wall or fence and perhaps a small lawn.

What you can have depends entirely on what you have time for, so address the two issues together and compromise wherever necessary.

what do you want?

Achieving a garden that will look good all year round, but take only an hour each week to maintain may mean making some quite fundamental changes to what is already there. Begin by deciding what you want from your garden. Use the questions below to identify the changes you need to make and the ways in which the existing layout should be adapted.

what do you want from your garden?

The first things to consider are how much time you can devote to maintaining your garden and what you really want from it. For example, do you want a place for private relaxation or do you plan to entertain in it? Do you need to provide a safe area for children to play or would you like an area to grow a few choice plants? Answer the following questions honestly to help you focus your mind on what you really need, what you would like to have and what you have time to do.

How do you plan to use the garden?

relaxing ◯   sunbathing ◯   playing games ◯   entertaining ◯   barbecues ◯   growing plants ◯

Who uses the garden?

adults ◯   children ◯   pets ◯

What features do you need to include?

tool shed ◯   storage for bicycles and toys ◯   washing line ◯   parking for a car ◯

space for dustbins ◯   play equipment for children ◯

What would you like to have?

space for outdoor dining ◯   somewhere to relax and sunbathe ◯   a shady place for sitting in warm weather ◯

a water feature ◯   somewhere to grow climbing plants ◯   a few easy-care edibles ◯

What type of garden would you like?

modern and minimal ◯   formal ◯   leafy and exuberant ◯   semi-wild ◯

How much time can you spare to tend the garden?

one hour a week or less ◯   one–two hours a week ◯   more than two hours a week ◯

How many plants do you want?

the bare minimum ◯   enough to make the garden interesting ◯   a good selection of different types ◯

▲ Decking makes a natural-looking surface that will look good in most gardens. Hardwood decking should last for many years.

first steps for change

When you have decided what you want from your garden, you can begin to look at the ways in which you can achieve those ends.

All gardens consist of a combination of hard surfaces and plants. Look at your own garden and look at the list of essential garden features (below). Creating a garden that can be maintained in an hour a week means choosing from among the available materials and features. If you have a wall – the ultimate no-care boundary – around all or a part of your garden, you could consider combining it with a surface such as bark chippings or even a lawn that will require more time and effort to maintain. Retaining an existing well-laid brick path, on the other hand, will save maintenance time that you might choose to spend on looking after a hedge.

essential garden features ••• no care •• little care • some easy care

paths
- ••• bricks
- ••• paving slabs
- •• gravel
- •• stepping stones
- • bark chippings

surfaces
- ••• concrete
- ••• paving
- •• meadow lawn
- •• decking
- •• gravel
- • bark chippings
- • traditional lawn

boundaries
- ••• closeboard fence
- •• open trellis or screen
- •• wooden gate
- • easy-care hedge
- • wrought iron gate

► Always ensure the features you introduce are easy-care.

optional extras ••• no care •• little care • some easy care

There are many ornamental features that you might want in your garden, and the planning process involves choosing among those that you would like and those that you have time to look after. If a water feature is important, for example, your choice of planting might be from the low-maintenance groundcover plants listed on pages 142–3; you may prefer to provide height and shade with a small tree rather than a wooden structure that will need annual maintenance.

uprights
- ••• small tree
- •• arch
- •• pergola
- •• gazebo
- •• obelisk
- •• screen

fillers
- ••• garden bench
- ••• garden ornament
- •• cobble fountain
- •• raised bed
- •• table and chairs
- • pond/water feature

plant features
- ••• groundcover
- •• ornamental grasses
- •• shrub border
- • containers
- • easy-care mixed border
- • easy edibles

do you really need a lawn?

What could be more attractive or more typical of a summer garden than an area of neatly mown, striped grass, sweeping down the garden in a graceful curve, with borders of colourful perennials tumbling over the edges in profuse abandon? Not a lot … unless you have to look after it.

▲ Lawns unify the whole design of a garden, and offer a space for sitting or playing in dry weather. They can be straight-sided or curved, depending on the design of the garden.

looking after the lawn

The flower-edged lawn, the archetypal image of a well-tended garden, is perhaps the most difficult of all features to maintain. The edge of a lawn that butts against a border or bed often crumbles away and looks untidy. You will be tempted to stand on the grass to get to the plants, wearing away the grass and weakening the structure of the soil beneath. By the end of summer the edge of the lawn will need to be repaired or a new edge cut. Where plants are allowed to billow over the lawn the grass does not grow properly and soon becomes bald, and bare patches in the grass will quickly be invaded by weeds and moss. Grass will grow down the edge of the lawn and into the border, where it cannot be reached by the mower, and it will have to be clipped with shears to keep it short or removed by hand.

In spring, grass will benefit from the application of weedkiller and fertilizer. These are available as combined 'weed and feed' preparations, which are comparatively simple to apply. A second application of fertilizer in summer is often recommended, and a third, autumn feed, designed to boost the grass before winter, can also be given.

Lawns also need regular aerating and scarifying. Aerating with a garden fork improves the drainage of the underlying soil, and scarifying with a spring-tined rake removes the thatch (dead grass) that always builds up over the season. These tasks are usually done in late summer or early autumn.

Moss can be a problem on badly drained lawns, and although chemicals can be used to kill the moss they will not improve the conditions that encouraged the moss to develop in the first place. Aerating and applying lawn sand will help.

In autumn fallen leaves must be swept up, and in early spring you may need to reseed worn areas or recut edges.

Don't forget that a lawn must be cut. To keep a lawn looking neat all summer long involves cutting it from early spring to late autumn if conditions allow, and during the summer months this task should be done once a week.

If you have no lawn, you will need no lawnmower, no spring-tined rake, no strimmer and no shears or half-moon edger. At a stroke, not only do you save hours every summer marching up and down the garden but you also cut down on your storage and maintenance requirements. Think carefully before you choose a lawn as a surface.

If you don't have a lawn, however, what are you going to replace it with? The surface will be the major feature in the garden, so this is a key decision in the initial planning process. Look at pages 30–35 for the pros and cons of the different surfaces.

▶ A hard edging, such as bricks, gravel or paving slabs set just below the edge of the lawn, allows the mower to pass over it and obviates the need for fiddly edge cutting.

save time

Given how much time and effort a lawn needs, it is perhaps surprising that anyone consciously decides to put part of their garden down to grass, but gardeners everywhere find it the perfect complement to plants and hard surfaces, as well as the ideal place for children to play safely. Grass can form absolutely any shape you want it to, including sweeping curves, circles and ovals. In an easy-care garden avoid the traditional rectangle of lawn with flowerbeds down each side and opt for something more interesting to transform your garden. Try a curving, irregular shape to add immediate interest to the design or even a simple circle, perhaps with the shape echoed in a circular seating area or pond elsewhere. You could even use the space to create two smaller lawns, separated by a screen of shrubs or a pond. Whatever shape you select, always avoid awkward angles and fussy curves in order to make life easier on yourself.

If you are one of the many gardeners who find that the advantages of a lawn outweigh the disadvantages, follow the five basic rules here to minimize the time you need to spend cutting the lawn each week in summer:

● Simplify the overall shape to make mowing less time consuming.

● Add a mowing strip all around the grass.

● Avoid island beds in the lawn: you will only have to mow round them.

● Remove features such as statues, sundials and birdbaths from the lawn and place them on the patio or on a plinth in a border.

● Make the edges relatively straight: smooth, shallow curves are acceptable, but lots of tight curves will make mowing and edging awkward.

do you need that planting space?

One of the fundamental aspects of planning a garden that can be maintained in a limited time is to reduce the proportion of the garden given over to plants. You may be unwilling to get rid of existing beds and borders in case the garden becomes drab and lifeless, but there are many ways to add interest and to make the plants that you do have really count.

easy-care alternatives to planting

Instead of devoting a large proportion of the garden to beds and borders, consider increasing the amount of garden that is given over to:

- Patios and paved areas: make sure that weeds cannot grow in the gaps between slabs or bricks.

- Hardwood decking: pressure-treated hardwood will last for many years without any maintenance.

- Large water features: a large, well-planted pond requires surprisingly little attention. Build a raised pool or fit a proper, secure edging that will last for many years.

- Brick or paving paths: well-built paths will last and provide a good framework for the rest of the garden. Make sure that weeds cannot grow between the paving.

▶ Although the ornamental grass in the pot will need watering, the rest of the plants in this area will take care of themselves.

planting solutions

It must be admitted that some of the best and most interesting gardens contain borders that require a fair amount of work to maintain, but there is no reason why you cannot create a border that is interesting all year round and that is easy to look after. The trade-off is simple: if you don't want to spend your life weeding, cutting back and attending to the borders, choose some easy-care plants and simplify your planting, spreading a mulch of cocoa shells or chipped

bark or even of gravel over your borders to hide the bare soil, conserve moisture and keep down weeds.

Take advantage of all the planting ideas that will help to minimize seasonal maintenance:

- Groundcover planting: covering bare soil is vital in the low-maintenance garden, and many plants will do the job effectively and attractively (see pages 84–5).

- Gravel garden: an area of gravel, laid over a weed-suppressing membrane, is a quick and cheap hard surface that will require nothing more than raking over from time to time.

- Chipped bark or cocoa shell borders: areas of this natural mulch, laid over a weed-suppressing membrane, provide easy-care and sympathetic surfaces for shrub borders and paths (see page 63).

- Low-labour lawns: grass is easier, on the whole, to maintain than flowerbeds and borders.

You should also consider making the existing borders narrower. This will give you easy access to the plants and enable you to reach them without standing on the soil and compacting it. This can cut down on maintenance in the long term because you won't have to dig over the soil to loosen it.

using shrubs

Shrubs, both evergreen and deciduous, are good choices for the one-hour gardener. Their eventual size means that they will take up a fair amount of space in a mixed border and provide a handsome backdrop for other plants. Make sure that you choose shrubs that require little care and that provide more than one season of interest, whether it is evergreen foliage, autumn colour, flowers or fruits (see pages 82–3 for some ideas for year-round colour).

Shrubs also make ideal focal points and can be used as specimen plants in their own right. They will add height and volume to a border and can be exploited for their architectural qualities or striking shapes.

value-for-money plants

When selecting plants for your easy-care garden, make sure you choose ones that will give good value, because they require no maintenance, provide a focal point or are useful groundcover, minimizing the amount of weeding.

- Choose some big, architectural plants, which will take up more space, thus reducing the number of individual plants you need, and make a bold statement in a border.

- Make sure your plants provide a range of different shapes and textures to compensate for there being fewer of them. Each one must really earn its space.

- Include a good number of foliage plants. These will be more effective in covering the soil and provide a longer season of interest than flowers. See pages 90–91 for some ideas for easy-care foliage plants.

- Although often regarded as being dull, conifers can create a good framework for a border, covering a fair amount of ground and blocking out light for weeds. Choose several different conifers to give different colours and shape and intersperse them with deciduous plants to give seasonal variation.

- Arrange plants in large drifts where possible. Several plants of the same type will have the same maintenance requirements. Many hardy perennials are suited to this treatment, and large groups will look effective.

- Use ornamental grasses to add height, texture, colour and seasonal interest. These are plants that will look after themselves but provide drama on a big scale.

- Don't forget to include evergreen trees, shrubs and perennials. These will form the basis of the border during winter.

◄ Ensure that plants are suitable for your conditions: this agave is tender and would require lifting in areas prone to cold winters.

making a plan

Once you have decided what you want from your garden and on its overall style you can begin to make your plan. Look at the gardens of friends and relatives for inspiration, but remember that your garden should not require endless hours spent on tedious, unnecessary jobs. Therefore, your new garden plan should not include:

- Paving with gaps in which weeds and annual seeds will grow
- Lawn edges that need cutting
- Hedges that require cutting more than once a year
- Shrubs, such as roses, that need pruning
- Annual bedding plants
- Plants that are susceptible to diseases
- Plants in a situation or soil that does not suit them
- Deciduous trees overhanging ponds or gravel
- Perennials that need regular staking, deadheading or dividing
- Over-vigorous plants that will quickly outgrow their allotted space

If any of these elements are present in your garden now, begin your plan by deciding on the best way to eradicate them. For example, if there is a lawn that butts against beds or borders consider adding an edging of paving stones or bricks to make mowing easier (see pages 132–3), and if you have large borders filled with summer bedding think about replacing these with reliable groundcover (see pages 84–5) or look at some of our ideas for effortless borders (see pages 80–81). As you prepare your new plan, making sure that you avoid the time-consuming features listed above, concentrate on a few simple 'golden' rules for your easy-care garden:

- Reduce the area devoted to planting
- Have as much paving, decking or gravel as possible
- If you must have a lawn, edge it with a mowing strip
- Don't leave any bare soil: either mulch it or use groundcover plants
- Avoid fast-growing hedges at all costs
- Choose reliable, easy-care plants that will be happy in the conditions you have

▲ This town garden makes use of easy-care paving, avoiding a lawn altogether and leaving a small area for planting.
▶ This small, shady garden includes a secret seating area for quiet contemplation. The decking and cushions add colour to the scene.

drawing up the plan

Although it may seem tedious and unnecessary, making a plan will help you see clearly what you already have and what you might have. It will not take long to complete, and although it's worth taking the trouble to get the dimensions correct you do not have to be an artist to sketch in the outlines of an established tree or a path.

1 Draw a scale plan of the garden as it is. Mark the positions of the existing features, such as trees, paths, boundaries and patios.

2 Take time to study the plan. It will be a useful guide to what space you have and what you can do to adapt the features that take up most of your time.

3 Choose a selection of features from the lists on page 17. Some will be things you have; others will be those that you need or would like to have. Don't choose just one surface type: the garden will be more interesting if you mix and match.

4 Play around with the plan to see how you can incorporate new features by replacing the old, labour-intensive ones.

5 When the new plan is complete, look again at your answers to the questions in the checklist on pages 12–13. Roughly estimate the time it will take you to maintain each element, and then see if the total coincides with the time you have decided you can spend on the garden. If it does not, replace one or more of the more time-consuming features with an easy-care option.

sun and shade

One of the key considerations when you are making a plan is the way sun and shade fall across the garden. This is important for patios and sitting areas – most people like sun for at least part of the day – but will also be important for planting areas. Many lovely plants revel in shade, but on the whole it is easier to choose easy-care subjects for a sunny position. Don't forget that areas of sun and shade move around during the day.

5 jobs to avoid

As you begin to draw up a new plan make sure that your new garden features do not introduce any of the following time-consuming tasks. Your aim is to avoid these jobs as far as you possibly can:

● weeding   ● hedge trimming

● lawn edge clipping

● digging   ● pruning

easy-care checklist

When you have made plans to simplify the design of the garden, ask yourself the following questions to make sure you have considered every point.

● Do the paths lead fairly directly to important features, such as the shed or compost heap?

● Are there any obstructions on the lawn that will hamper easy mowing?

● Does the patio get sun for at least some of the day?

● Are the paths wide enough for wheelbarrows or pushchairs?

● Is the paved area large enough for a table and chairs or whatever you plan to use it for?

● Are there any overhanging trees that will drop leaves into ponds or on to gravel areas?

● Have you left space for the essentials, such as a washing line, tool shed, space to place the dustbins or somewhere to store garden furniture?

boundary solutions

All gardens need some kind of boundary to provide privacy and security, and you will probably have to choose from walls, hedges and fences. Although walls and fences require the least care, hedges, too, can be planted to minimize maintenance, and if minimizing noise, whether from your neighbours or a nearby road, is important, a hedge is likely to be your first choice.

In addition to marking the boundary of your property, these vertical elements can also be used within the garden to divide it up, to add height or to provide somewhere to grow climbers.

▲ Stone makes an ideal material for low walls around raised beds or between the levels of terraces as it will not deteriorate when it comes in contact with damp soil.

choosing a boundary

A good boundary should act as a visual backdrop to the garden, bringing together the overall design and showing off plants and elements within it. Treat walls, hedges and fences as garden elements like any others; they can be used to create an interesting and colourful feature in their own right.

Most gardens will already have a boundary. If your garden is bordered by a sturdy fence or wall, make the most of what you've got. These are useful, low-maintenance boundaries which can be made more attractive if needs be.

walls

Walls made from brick, stone or concrete blocks can be expensive to build, and if used as boundaries they will need to be fairly tall, making the cost even greater. However, they can be handsome features, which will last almost indefinitely, and are ideal for the gardener with limited time.

If you already have walls around your garden, consider yourself fortunate. You can always improve them by adding plants or other decorative elements (see page 59). If you are having a new wall built, choose the material carefully; there will be a large expanse of it and it will be there a long time. Natural stone and good-quality bricks are the best but most expensive options, but good barriers can be built using cheaper bricks or concrete blocks. Check local planning regulations governing the height of permanent boundaries, especially those bordering roads, and seek professional help if the wall is going to be higher than about 1m (3ft).

boundary pros and cons

••• no care   •• little care   • some easy care

style of boundary	pros	cons	tips
wall •••	Provides instant cover Provides shelter for plants Long lasting	Expensive to build	Choose plain bricks or natural stone and a classic design that will not date
fence ••	Provides instant cover Relatively cheap to erect	Will need replacing eventually Can be an unattractive orange-brown	Use pressure-treated timber
trellis ••	Cheap to erect Makes a less solid divider Will support plants	Will need replacing eventually Unsuitable for use alone as an external boundary	Use pressure-treated timber
hedge •	Natural, leafy appearance Absorbs sound well	Needs clipping at least once a year Takes time to mature	Use slow-growing shrubs to create an informal hedge

style solutions for walls

● Brick is available in many different colours, depending on the clay used in their manufacture, and there is usually an attractive variation in tone, creating walls with interesting, uneven colour. It is an especially suitable choice if the wall can echo the bricks used for the house. Bricks are easy to lay and use and can be extended to raised beds, patios and barbecues.

● Natural stone walls are strong, bold features, which can be built up to about 1.8m (6ft) tall. They look best when local stone is used, particularly if the house is built of the same material. Like brick, the stones are held in place with mortar. Stone walls are generally expensive, but they can make beautiful features, especially if small plants are allowed to grow between the stones.

● Dry stone walls are usually lower than mortared stone walls. They look most suitable in rural gardens in areas where the stone is local. They can look rather incongruous in town gardens. Dry stone walling is a skill, which should be left to experienced craftsmen.

● Concrete blocks are large units, which can be used as a solid wall or to give a honeycomb pattern. They are cheap, strong and easy to use, and can be rendered with cement for a smooth finish, painted or left plain if they are attractive enough. Concrete blocks are good in modern settings and can be used to create a host of different effects.

▼ *Clematis* 'Ascotiensis' and *Rosa* 'Parkdirektor Riggers' are trained up this plain brick wall and allowed to grow through each other freely to create an area of vivid colour.

fences, trellis and screens

Fences, trellis and screens are relatively quick and cheap to erect, and they make instant and generally effective boundaries and dividers. There is a wide range of materials and styles available, and you will have no difficulty in finding something suitable for your garden.

As with all wooden features used outside, they must be constructed properly if they are going to last. Cheap fences look like cheap fences and will soon start to deteriorate. Buy the best you can afford and make sure it is adequately protected with wood preservative.

Unlike more solid fences, trellis is generally too lightweight to be an effective external boundary, but it is ideal for dividing different areas of the garden because it allows glimpses of what is beyond. It is also an effective means of extending the height of a fence without creating a looming, solid barrier. Trellis panels, which are available in several patterns, can be attached to walls and fences to support climbing plants.

▲ Thin bamboo canes make a good decorative fence for an informal garden. The heavier horizontal rails serve to emphasize the delicacy of the uprights.

▶ Trellis screens can be made more private by the addition of climbing plants, like this *Parthenocissus quinquefolia*. However, this plant, like many climbers, loses its leaves in winter, so if you want year-round cover choose an evergreen climber.

making it last

Buying good-quality timber will greatly increase the lifespan of a fence or wooden screen. The most important consideration is to check that the timber has been pressure-treated with a preservative. Choose good-quality hardwood wherever possible; softwood can be used but will need to be treated with a wood preservative every year or two to keep it protected against the weather, rot and pests.

style solutions for fences

- Panel fences are made from individual panels, usually 1.8m (6ft) long and 0.90–1.8m (3–6ft) high. They are made of thin, woven strips of wood held by a sturdy frame. They are best used as an unobtrusive backdrop, using their uniformity to advantage. Avoid the cheap, garish orange-brown panels, or stain them a darker brown or green to tone them down.

- Closeboard fences are similar in style to panel fences but are constructed from boards nailed vertically to a framework, creating a strong and solid boundary. They are generally more expensive than panel fences, but are better suited to slopes and can be fitted around trees and other obstructions.

- Picket fences, popular in cottage gardens, are generally fairly low. They consist of a series of vertical planks with gaps between, fixed to horizontal rails. They make attractive barriers within the garden or can be used around a front garden where privacy is not essential.

- Post-and-rail fences are cheap to erect but create a rather stark boundary, offering no privacy or security. They are suitable in country gardens, where they mark a boundary while maintaining a view.

- Bamboo canes can be used to make solid screens, and fine canes are available laced together in panel form. Thicker canes can make more open fences, with the canes arranged vertically or diagonally.

▲ Broader bamboo canes make attractive and solid boundaries for a modern, formal or oriental setting.

- Wattle hurdles are made from flexible willow or hazel stems woven together. They are becoming increasingly popular and will create a solid and natural-looking boundary or divider. If they are sturdily made they should last for about ten years.

- Trellis is usually made in panels with horizontal and vertical bars creating a squared effect, but there are many other patterns available. It makes a fine divider between areas of the garden but is not really suited to forming an external boundary because it is too see-through. It makes a good support for climbing plants and these will help to create a more solid barrier.

choosing a fence

type of fence	privacy	appearance	support for plants	longevity
bamboo	good	good	not good	not good
closeboard	very good	not bad	good	good
panel fence	very good	not bad	good	good
picket fence	not much	very good	low plants only	good
post and rail	none	not bad	none	good
trellis	not much	good	very good	not bad
wattle hurdles	very good	very good	good	not bad

hedges

Hedges are probably the most labour-intensive form of barrier, but they have many advantages that make them worth considering. They absorb sound better than fences, prevent pollution passing through from busy roads and create a more natural, leafy backdrop to the garden. Although they do need to be trimmed regularly, choosing a slow-growing evergreen hedge, or an informal hedge that will also give you the benefit of seasonal flowers, means this task can be limited to once a year.

If you already have a fast-growing hedge as a boundary, you will have to accept that you will be clipping it several times each year or replace it with something more manageable, but think carefully before removing a mature hedge that will have taken many years to establish.

Whatever you do, avoid the common fast-growing hedging plants. *Chamaecyparis lawsoniana* (Lawson cypress) and, worse still, x *Cupressocyparis leylandii* (Leyland cypress) need trimming at least three times during the growing season to keep them in check, and even *Ligustrum ovalifolium* (privet) needs clipping twice a year to keep it neat. If the hedge is going to be reasonably long also avoid broad-leaved hedging plants, such as *Prunus lusitanica* (Portugal laurel), which are not suited to trimming with powered hedge-trimmers.

top 10 hedging plants

	formal/ informal	deciduous/ evergreen	cutting time	features
Berberis darwinii (barberry)	i	e	after flowering in late spring	glossy leaves and orange flowers
Carpinus betulus (hornbeam)	f	d	mid- to late summer	similar to beech
Crataegus monogyna (hawthorn)	i	d	winter	white blossom and spiny stems
Escallonia cvs.	i	e	after flowering in summer	red or pink flowers
Fagus sylvatica (beech)	f	d	late summer	retains brown leaves through winter
Ilex aquifolium (common holly)	f	e	late summer	green or variegated leaves and red berries
Pyracantha rogersiana (firethorn)	i	e	after fruiting	white flowers and orange-red berries
Rosa rugosa (hedgehog rose)	i	e	spring	large pink flowers and red rose hips
Taxus baccata (yew)	f	e	summer	makes a dense, dark green screen
Thuja plicata (western red cedar)	f	e	spring	slow-growing conifer

save time

- Choose appropriate plants for the hedge to minimize any maintenance needed.

- Use an electric or petrol-driven hedge-trimmer. Although this is only a once-a-year job, the time saved more than makes up for the cost. If you don't want to buy a hedge-trimmer hire one when you need it.

- Plant groundcover or lay a thick mulch under the hedge to avoid having to weed in such a difficult place.

- Maintain access to the hedge for easier clipping. Don't plant other plants right up against it.

hedge care plan

If you have chosen slow-growing hedging plants, follow this care plan:

- Cut the hedge once a year to maintain its shape.

- Feed the hedge once a year to keep it healthy. Sprinkle a slow-release fertilizer under the hedge and fork it in lightly.

- Water thoroughly in dry weather until the hedge is established. Shallow watering encourages shallow roots, which are susceptible to drought.

container-grown hedges for instant effect

Hedges require proper soil preparation at planting time to get them off to a good start. If you don't fancy the hard work, plant a container-grown hedge instead. These are most suitable as dividers and edgings rather than as garden boundaries, but they can be as tall as the size of your containers will allow. Use a row of identical containers, large enough for the plants you want to use, and fill them with a good-quality, soil-based compost. Arrange the tubs in a neat row, evenly spaced, and plant the shrubs in them. *Lavandula* (lavender), *Buxus* (box), *Santolina* (cotton lavender) or any of the hedging plants in the table opposite can be used. Mulch the tops of the containers to retain moisture and trim the plants to keep them neat.

▼ Box (*Buxus*) and yew (*Taxus baccata*) grow slowly and are ideal for low-maintenance hedging.

surface solutions

In most gardens the area of patio, paving or decking is limited, but hard surfaces provide a secure, dry space for outdoor dining, barbecues, sunbathing, relaxing and hobbies, and most people would find a use for a bit more. What's more, increasing the area of the hard surfaces will simplify the design of the easy-maintenance garden, giving you less 'garden' to worry about. A large area of paving or decking need not be dull: all you need to do is to make the paving itself more interesting – add permanent features, such as a raised bed or bench, or introduce a few large, strategically placed containers.

choosing surfaces

Because patios, paths and decks are usually the major features in a garden, decisions about the materials you use and the way you lay them should come early on in the planning process. Some surfaces, such as paving slabs, require no attention at all after they have been laid, but they are more difficult to lay in the first place. At the other end of the scale are surfaces like grass, which are comparatively inexpensive and easy to put down but which need to be looked after from then on. The style of the garden you wish to create and your budget will probably be the overriding factors in your choice, but the next few pages give extra advice on ways to cut down on unnecessary later work.

▲ Bricks make handsome and hard-wearing paths. They are available in a range of different colours and can be laid in a variety of patterns.

paths

Within the garden, paths can be made from any of the materials used for larger areas of hard surface, and the same considerations apply. Try to tie the paths in with the rest of the garden by using the same materials as for the patio or seating area, or a variation that complements the other materials used. Gravel or bark paths need to be edged in some way to prevent the loose material spreading. If the path borders the lawn, a brick or timber mowing strip will take care of the problem; if the path runs adjacent to a border, you have a much wider choice of edgings, many of them decorative.

top 5 easy-care surfaces

The one-hour garden will contain surfaces created from one or more of the following materials. Combining surfacing materials is a useful way of breaking up what could be rather dull areas.

- Paving slabs
- Block pavers or bricks
- Concrete
- Hardwood decking
- Gravel laid over a weed-suppressing membrane

▲ This path is a colourful feature in its own right, cutting a curved course through the planting rather like a river.

hard surfaces ••• no care •• little care • some easy care

material	pros	cons	tips
paving slabs •••	Maintenance free Durable Natural stone is attractive	Expensive to buy and hard work to lay Artificial slabs can be gaudy	Choose natural colours for a sympathetic look
bricks and pavers •••	Maintenance free Durable and attractive	Fiddly to lay Can be expensive	Choose frostproof brick
concrete •••	Inexpensive and easy to lay Maintenance free Durable and fits any space	Can look stark and featureless	Use for small areas only Brush the surface before it dries to reveal the aggregate
gravel ••	Inexpensive and easy to lay Available in a range of colours and sizes Burglar deterrent	May need topping up and raking from time to time Weeds can emerge through it	Create an edge to contain the gravel Lay a weed-suppressing membrane
bark chips ••	Easy to lay Soft surface for children	Can be expensive May need occasional topping up	Create an edge to contain the bark Lay a weed-suppressing membrane
decking ••	Can be laid on awkward or uneven surfaces Fairly long lasting Little maintenance required	Relatively expensive Will eventually need renewing	Use pressure-treated hardwood
grass •	Looks natural Soft surface for children Inexpensive and easy to lay	Needs regular mowing Unusable in winter	Choose a hard-wearing rye grass mixture for lower maintenance

concrete

Although it has a reputation for being dull, concrete can be used imaginatively to create a sympathetic, attractive surface. It can be laid to any shape, allowing great flexibility of design, and provides a hard-wearing surface. The appearance of the surface depends on the aggregate used in the mixture, so it is possible to create a wide variety of effects. The mixture can be allowed to dry smooth or can be brushed as it dries to expose the pebbles in it. It is also possible to colour concrete with special dyes, which is useful in modern gardens.

paving

Paving, which includes slabs, bricks and pavers, is the most durable of surface materials and will last indefinitely if laid properly. Although it can be expensive to buy and rather hard to lay, once in place paving requires no maintenance at all. Large areas of a uniform surface can be rather featureless, but a little thought during the planning process can produce an attractive surface that looks good all year. Some ideas for laying paving and for creating decorative effects are given on pages 44–5.

▲ Paving is suitable for paths and patios. Slabs are often square, but other shapes, such as rectangles, are available for a more interesting, sympathetic look.

save time with paving

- Lay paving materials on a firm base of compacted hardcore so you will not need to repair or replace the surface for some years.

- Point the gaps between the paving stones with mortar so that no weeds can become established. Alternatively, plant small carpeting plants in the gaps to suppress the weeds and create a softer look.

- Avoid laying paving under deciduous trees or you will have to clear up the leaves in autumn.

- Always choose frostproof paving materials to save time on repairs later on.

- Lay the paving on a slight slope to ensure good drainage. This will avoid future problems with standing water.

decking

Decking is a versatile material, which can be used to create a surface of any shape, making it a useful design solution. It is warm and comfortable to walk on, and a properly laid deck will last for many years. Being lightweight and easy to lay, decking is the perfect surface for roof gardens and balconies, but it is also an excellent cover for uneven surfaces because the subframe can easily be adapted to accommodate uneven ground without the need for time-consuming levelling. Decking, however, can be expensive, especially if you use hardwood.

For a long-lasting surface use strong timber for the subframe and durable hardwood for the boards themselves. All the timber should be pressure-treated with preservative to prevent it rotting. Hardwood is more expensive than softwood but will last many more years and will not need a yearly application of preservative after the initial one. Check, however, that the hardwood comes from a renewable source to avoid further destruction of tropical rainforests. Use galvanized screws, nails or bolts to fix the decking together as they will not rust.

Decking can also be bought in pre-made squares, usually 60 x 60cm (2 x 2ft), which are a bit like paving slabs. These can be used as stepping stones or laid on a framework of closely laid struts to form a deck. They are perfect for roof gardens as they can be simply laid in position without the need for nailing, but the underlaying surface must be flat or the tiles will rock.

▲ Decking can be stained in a host of different colours, such as this cool grey-lilac, to create whatever effect you desire.

◄ Decking makes a sturdy and stylish path. Here the planks have been laid in a diagonal pattern which looks very effective but would require a lot of cutting to lay.

decking extras

● Build handrails around the deck to enclose a decked dining area. This is an attractive addition to a deck and is essential on high-level decks.

● Add a timber pergola over the deck and grow scented climbers or a grape vine over it.

● Incorporate raised timber beds into the design to surround your deck with flowers.

● Cut a few holes in a low-level deck to accommodate some shrubs or large perennials planted in the ground underneath. A deck can be built around the trunk of an existing tree or treasured shrub if needs be.

● Build the deck on two levels for added interest.

● Incorporate some timber steps up to the deck.

● Add built-in bench seating to the design and include some colourful, removable cushions to be brought out when the seats are in use.

gravel

Using gravel as a surface for a path or as mulch in a border is an ideal low-maintenance solution, especially when it is laid over a semi-permeable weed-suppressing membrane, which allows water to penetrate to the soil below but prevents perennial weeds from growing up. Annual weeds are easily removed because they cannot get their roots down through the membrane. It is an ideal material for putting around plants because it conserves moisture and warmth in the ground.

Gravel is available in a range of colours and sizes, and the colours are enhanced by rainwater. It is easy to put down, and is also easy to lift and use elsewhere in the garden if wanted.

The drawbacks are that gravel 'travels'. Make sure that the area is well edged so that chippings do not get onto the lawn (they can be dangerous if they are picked up by the lawnmower) or even into the house if they get trapped in the soles of gardening shoes. It is also a hard surface to fall on, so if you have children, chipped bark would be a good alternative.

◄ Coarse greystone chips set off these conifers well and bring out the blue tones in the foliage.
▼ Gravel makes a sympathetic and pleasing surface for a large area, especially if you choose pea shingle in a neutral colour.

which kind of gravel?

The word gravel is used for a variety of surfacing materials, each appropriate and useful in different places:

- Coarse-grade stone chippings, either limestone or granite, can be used loose; they are available in a range of colours, from pure white through cool grey to warm golden-brown. Slate is also available in large chippings.

- Shingle has a finer texture; pea shingle has rounded edges, which makes it a more suitable surface for areas where children play, and fine-textured, washed shingle is an ideal topping for containers.

- Horticultural grit is useful as a mulch, although it is so fine that it is soon washed into the soil.

▶ Bark chippings are comfortable to walk on and will form a natural-looking path for a woodland garden.

bark chippings

Bark chippings and crushed cocoa shell are natural materials that bring a warm, woodland feel to a garden or border. These materials can be used to make an informal path or seating area, to cover the soil under shrubs or to provide a soft landing under children's play equipment.

They are ideal for using as a mulch around all types of plants, but they look most at home in a shady border, where they can be used to cover the soil under mixed shrubs and a few choice foliage plants, such as hostas and ferns. They suppress weeds by preventing light from reaching the soil beneath. For a really labour-free surface, however, lay heavy-duty plastic sheeting or a weed-suppressing membrane underneath and contain the material with a timber edging to hold it in place.

Bark chippings are an appropriate infill material when railway sleepers are used as an edging for steps or raised beds. If logs are used to edge an area, use timber pegs on both sides to hold the logs in position. Large log slices can be used as stepping stones spaced at easy intervals through the mulch. Chippings are an ideal companion for natural-coloured decking, which can be used to provide a firm area for a table and chairs, and they also go well with wooden furniture, pergolas and arches.

which type of chippings?

- Bark chippings are, as the name suggests, simply pieces of chipped bark. They come in a range of sizes, from fine, suitable as a mulch, to much coarser material, which can be used to create a surface to walk on.

- Composted bark is a softer material that is more suitable for use as a soil conditioner, but it can be used as a mulch in a shrub or woodland border.

- Cocoa shell, a reddish-brown material with a rich, chocolate scent, has a neater, more regular appearance than bark chippings, and it is rather more expensive.

- Wood chippings are much paler in colour than bark chippings but can be used to create a similar effect. Again, they are available in a range of grades, from fine to coarse.

create it

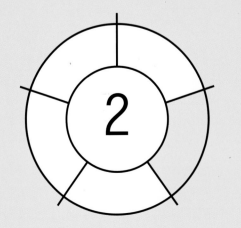

There are many different garden styles to choose from and some are, by their nature, easier to look after than others. Shrub gardens, gravel gardens and outdoor rooms, for example, require little maintenance, relying on proportionately large areas of labour-saving surfaces and easy-care plants. The low-maintenance gardener will naturally opt for one of the styles that are easy to care for and avoid others, such as the cottage garden, where the natural exuberance of the planting belies the careful and expert management that is needed to maintain it in good condition.

Although changing your garden to one that can, with the minimum of supervision, look after itself may take some time, hard work and forward planning, there are some things that will make a big difference for relatively little effort. Some of these are discussed in the first half of this chapter, which features a number of 'quick fix' treatments that will bring instant improvement. If you have a large garden, these

solutions can be applied to a small section within the overall area so that you have more time to concentrate on other areas or features.

The second part of the chapter focuses on six 'off-the-peg' designs. These projects, each of which is accompanied by a simple plan, show how the elements discussed in the first chapter and the quick fix solutions described in the first part of this chapter can be brought together to create a garden with an individual character. Having a low-maintenance garden does not mean that you cannot impose your own style and preferences on it. These designs, which range from a calm stone and gravel garden, reminiscent of an oriental garden, to a leafy jungle garden, suggest ways in which surfaces, boundaries and planting schemes can be combined to create different effects. You can adapt these designs for your own garden or adjust them to suit your own preferences and lifestyle by introducing other, easy-care features highlighted in other schemes.

'having a low-maintenance garden does not mean that you cannot impose your own style and preferences on it'

◄ Plain wooden fencing and trellis can be transformed through the use of woodstain to create a modern, stylish boundary.

▲ Paving and decking have been combined to
create a natural-looking surface in this shady garden.

simple makeover: from overgrown plot to no-maintenance garden

Unless you have a brand-new plot that you can plan from scratch you will probably have inherited a garden from the previous owners who may not have been concerned to design a garden with easy upkeep in mind. Indeed, the garden will have slipped into a state of partial dereliction if it has proved too time-consuming to keep up. **care rating ●●●**

before

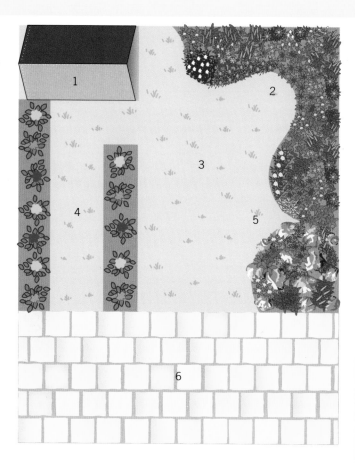

1 unappealing shed
2 mixed flowerbed
3 lawn
4 rose beds
5 high-maintenance rock garden
6 small slab patio

This small, square garden in a fairly shady position has several unappealing features as well as many time-consuming ones. The most noticeable features are the rose beds, which are badly sited and require high maintenance. Roses do not flower well in shade, the bare soil around the shrubs needs constant weeding and roses, of course, need pruning. The no-maintenance gardener will take immediate steps to get rid of the roses. The flower bed, too, has many small plants, with lots of bare soil showing around them, ready to be colonized by weeds, which are difficult to remove from between the plants. The shape of the border makes mowing difficult, and some of the plants are sun-lovers and will not thrive in a shaded corner.

The lawn is another feature that will require attention, because grass does not grow well in shade and the many edges need regular clipping. The rock garden, too, is a high-maintenance feature, requiring regular weeding.

save time

- Choose plants that require no pruning. Make sure they are shade-lovers that will thrive in this garden and pick at least some evergreens for year-round interest.

- Lay a weed-suppressing membrane under the gravel or you will be constantly weeding.

- Choose a good-quality bench so you will not have to replace it too soon.

- Use mortar between the slabs to prevent weed growth.

after

Applying a coat of lilac woodstain to the dull brown shed has lightened and brightened the garden, and a colourful blue bench has been placed at the far end of the garden to provide a focal point from the patio and somewhere pleasant to sit and admire the garden. The floor of the garden has been covered with a weed-suppressing membrane, over which a thick mulch of gravel has been laid. The leafy shrubs that have been planted through the membrane will require little attention. The enlarged patio is continued by the use of paving slabs as stepping stones that wind through the gravel to the bench, unifying the two sections of the layout. One of the paving slabs has been lifted from the patio and a shrub planted in the hole.

Making these simple changes means no more pruning and feeding roses or spraying them to prevent blackspot, no more weeding awkward flowerbeds and rock gardens, no more mowing the lawn and trimming the edges and no more nursing sun-loving plants in a shady border.

1 shed stained with lilac
2 garden bench stained blue to add colour
3 leafy, shade-loving shrubs planted through gravel
4 small group of plants planted in gravel
5 ceramic balls to add colour and interest
6 gravel area laid over a weed-suppressing membrane
7 stepping stones
8 paving slab has been removed to accommodate shrub
9 enlarged patio

woodstain

Brightly coloured woodstains have made a relatively recent appearance but have taken the garden scene by storm. No longer do we have to find ways to hide a dull brown shed or suffer a dreary closeboard fence at the back of a border. The application of a coat of woodstain – now available in aerosol sprays for even easier use – will transform a shed into a positive feature of which you will be proud, and turn the fence into an attractive backdrop to your border that will enhance the plants and show them off to their best advantage. It will also provide colour even when the plants are not in flower.

The colour or colours you choose will have a big effect in creating a style and imposing a character on the garden. How far you can go will depend on your surroundings, but avoid shocking colours in relatively natural-looking gardens. If you have an urban garden you can exercise your imagination to the full, especially if it is one with plenty of paving or decking.

▲ If it is impossible to hide a utilitarian building such as a shed, make a feature of it by painting it, for instance, lilac.

simple makeover: from boring plot to low-maintenance garden

This is a long garden with a difficult, shady alley down one side that has been emphasized by the narrow flowerbed and the dog-leg extension of the crazy paving on the patio.

Most gardens will contain at least some features that are worth keeping, and you should think before you remove established features. If you rip everything out in a moment of despair you will be left with a bare, featureless plot. You may be able to incorporate some things, perhaps in an altered form, into the new design. Try to keep any large trees or shrubs unless there are good reasons to remove them, as it can take large plants many years to look really established. **care rating** ●●●

before

In addition to the long, narrow flowerbeds against the two opposite walls, the garden is unnecessarily divided by a fast-growing hedge, which hides the large shed and vegetable plot from the patio. The lawn needs edging after every mowing so that the grass does not grow in the flowerbeds. The patio is too small to accommodate a table and chairs, and in any case the crazy paving is uneven. The stones surrounding the pond have been laid so that grass and weeds can grow between them, and tucked in the corner behind the pond is an almost completely inaccessible flowerbed.

1 shed – larger than necessary
2 vegetable patch with bare soil between plants
3 gate
4 fast-growing hedge
5 flowerbed
6 lawn
7 long flowerbed
8 crazy paving
9 pond
10 inaccessible flowerbed

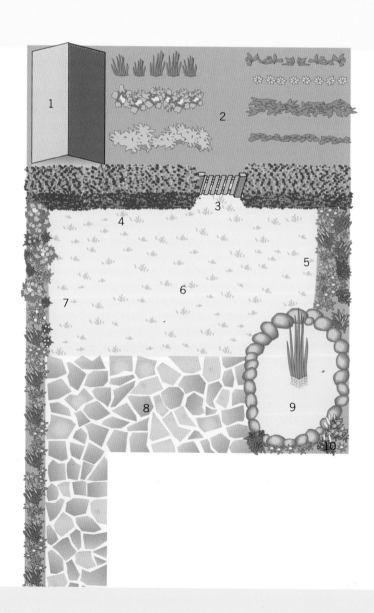

after

The first change has been to extend the area of patio by laying decking, which not only provides a large, level area that takes up more space and eliminates awkward corners but, by being laid at an angle, makes the narrow section by the side of the house look wider. The decking has been cut so that it provides a neat, overhanging edge to the pond. Long, narrow flowerbeds have been replaced by climbers growing in containers against trellises and shaped beds that make the space look less static. A brick-built raised bed provides an alternative, easy-maintenance container for vegetables, and this and a small garden store are partially hidden from view by a trellis clothed with a climber. The lawn has been completely edged with a mowing strip of bricks that match those used for the raised bed. The area on the far side of the lawn has been covered with a weed-suppressing membrane over which a layer of gravel has been laid, and a few architectural plants have been planted through the membrane. In the flowerbed some easy-care shrubs and perennials have been grouped close together to stop weeds becoming established.

Making these changes gives a low-maintenance garden that eliminates weeding and cutting back large flowerbeds, clipping lawn edges, cutting the hedge, back-breaking digging in the vegetable patch, weeding and trimming grass between the pond edging stones, pruning shrubs in the borders and trying to get plants to survive in a narrow, dry border in deep shade.

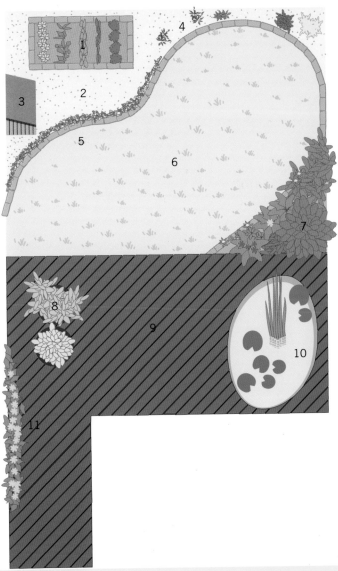

1 raised brick bed
2 gravel laid over a weed-suppressing membrane
3 garden store for tools
4 architectural foliage plants and grasses planted into the gravel
5 trellis with colourful climbers
6 lawn with brick mowing-strip
7 small border with a few easy-care plants
8 containers with permanent foliage plants
9 large area of hardwood decking
10 pond
11 shade-loving climber

▲ *(right)* Decking and water have a natural affinity. Be sure to include some aquatic plants in the pond to soften the effect.

quick fix: from lawn to paving

Almost every garden needs a level, hard surface next to the house, and replacing an existing lawn or part of it with paving slabs is not a difficult job, but it is one that will save future time and effort in lawn maintenance.

Of course, if you can manage without it, it is better to do away with the lawn altogether. This is especially true in small, shady gardens, where the grass will be lank and sparse from lack of light, and the bald patches will be made worse by constant wear in the same places. Transforming it into an area of paving will give you a firm, all-weather surface that does not need regular mowing, trimming or feeding. **care rating ●●●**

▲ Paving can be made more exciting by the use of plants growing in the gaps. These pretty campanulas will fill the spaces and prevent weeds growing.

planting in the gaps

If you do not want a uniformly hard, severe surface, fill the gaps between the paving slabs with plants rather than pointing with mortar. Lay the slabs in the usual way, but fill the gaps with a mixture of sand and sieved soil. Plant small carpeting plants in the gaps to give the paving a softer look and prevent weeds growing. Choose plants such as *Thymus serpyllum* (creeping thyme), camomile or *Soleirolia soleirolii* (baby's tears), which will not mind being trodden on occasionally.

what's wrong with lawns?

A well-maintained lawn always looks attractive, providing the perfect foil for plants of all types, but achieving a dense carpet of even, level sward is hard work. In addition to regular mowing, a lawn has to be fed, weeded, brushed clear of fallen leaves, raked to remove thatch and moss, and aerated. Moreover, a lawn that butts against beds or borders has to be edged regularly to keep the long grass clipped and the edges crisp and neat.

what's good about paving?

Paving provides a firm, level surface on which tables, chairs and sunloungers can be stood. It is usable all year round, no matter what the weather, and the huge range of colours, shapes and materials available means that the paving can be laid in eye-catching designs and patterns that, if wished, can continue the décor from inside the house to help foster the illusion of the outdoor room. Apart from the occasional brush to remove leaves and other debris, properly laid paving, with no cracks to provide space for weeds, is the ultimate no-maintenance surface.

Replacing lawn with paving means no more mowing the grass, no more clipping the edges, no more feeding and weeding the lawn and no more lawnmower to clutter up the shed or garage.

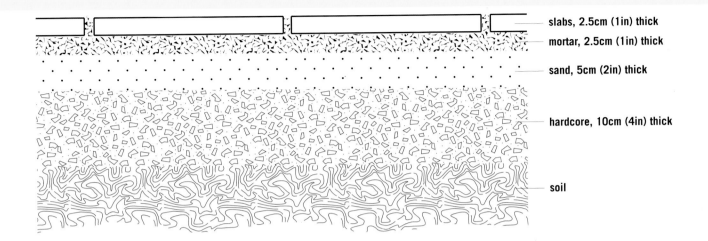

slabs, 2.5cm (1in) thick
mortar, 2.5cm (1in) thick
sand, 5cm (2in) thick
hardcore, 10cm (4in) thick
soil

how it's done

1 Remove the grass and underlying soil to a depth of 18cm (7in) plus the depth of the slabs. Take care not to loosen the subsoil and remember to incorporate a slight slope to allow rainwater to run off. If the paving adjoins the house wall, make sure the paving slopes away from the house. You may need to dig it out deeper next to the house: check building regulations for the minimum height required between the damp-proof course and the top of the paving.

2 Spread a 10cm (4in) layer of hardcore over the subsoil and compact it well to form a firm base.

3 Spread a 5cm (2in) layer of sand on top and, again, compact it well.

4 Bed the paving slabs on a layer of mortar on top of the sand base. Check the level of the slabs as you work to make sure they are aligned with their neighbours and make a flat, even surface. Allow the mortar to dry.

5 Point the gaps between the slabs with a mix of sand and cement to prevent weed growth.

decorative touches

● Mix slabs of different colours and textures to make the paving less featureless.

● Use slabs of different sizes so that the pattern is less regular. Natural stone comes in differing sizes anyway, but many man-made slabs are also available in a range of sizes. Work out the layout on paper before you buy, or you may end up with too many of one size and too few of another.

● Create interest by leaving out the odd slab. Fill the gaps with gravel or coloured glass chippings, or with cobbles or sets, which can be set into mortar. The gaps can also be used as planting holes for a few choice shrubs or perennials.

● Mix paving slabs with bricks for variety. Use the bricks as edging, as infills in gaps or as lines or patterns running through the paving.

● Lay basic square slabs in a variety of patterns to add interest. A checkerboard pattern is traditional, or you could arrange the slabs in staggered rows or at 45-degree angles to create a diagonal effect.

quick fix: from uneven ground to decking

A simple area of decking can hide a multitude of sins, and its great advantage over many other hard surfaces is that you don't have the back-breaking work of levelling the ground before you can lay it. When the decking is laid on short posts concreted into the ground, the deck will stand above the surface and you won't see what's underneath. It's the perfect surface to cover an area of broken paving or uneven, stony ground, and it is easily laid with the minimum of woodworking skills.

care rating ●●

what's wrong with uneven ground?

Few gardens are perfectly flat, but a garden that is on a noticeable slope poses particular challenges to the low-maintenance gardener. A lawn that slopes is difficult and tiring to mow, even with a hover mower and such an area cannot be covered with gravel or bark chippings. Decking is the ideal solution, providing, perhaps, an additional seating area in a part of the garden that you have not been able to use before. If you are laying decking over an existing old patio, there is no need to lift the slabs as they should provide a stable surface.

◄ Decking is the perfect surface if you want to cover up some slightly uneven paving or an unsightly concrete area. Simply lay the decking tiles or planks, on top of the hard surface.

decks on slopes

The structure of a deck lends itself perfectly to being built on a slope because the length of the uprights can be varied to accommodate the uneven ground. For a large, high-level deck, however, you may want to consider supporting the deck on brick piers instead of timber uprights.

Decking can extend out from a high point in the garden or be built to jut out over a large pond, but for more adventurous projects it would be sensible to get a professional to build the deck for you unless you are sure you have the necessary skills.

what's good about decking?

Decking is a sympathetic surface in the garden. It is pleasant to walk on and is not as unyielding as concrete or paving if it is used by children as a play area. It blends in well with planting of all kinds, and it looks especially appropriate near water. It can be cut to any shape, including curves, and can be laid in a variety of geometric patterns. It is particularly useful as a means of covering up uneven ground or making use of an awkward sloping area.

a raised deck: how it's done

1 Concrete a series of posts into the ground to form the uprights. Use a spirit level to make sure the tops of the posts are level. Use sacks of ready-mixed post concrete to speed up the process.

2 Fix a framework of joists to the uprights using bolts and galvanized brackets. These will support the boards.

3 Use galvanized nails or screws to fasten the wooden boards to the joists to make the deck. Leave a narrow but consistent gap between the boards: the gap should be wide enough to allow rainwater to drain between them but not so wide that the legs of chairs and tables get caught in the gaps.

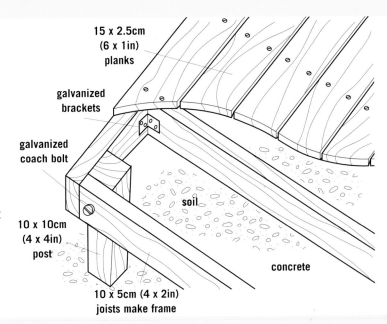

15 x 2.5cm (6 x 1in) planks
galvanized brackets
galvanized coach bolt
soil
10 x 10cm (4 x 4in) post
concrete
10 x 5cm (4 x 2in) joists make frame

decorative touches

- Stain the deck in subdued colours, such as moss green, soft grey or grey-blue, for an elegant effect that will complement surrounding plants.

- Use stronger colours, such as yellow, lilac or blue, for an eye-catching feature that will make the garden bright and colourful even in the depths of winter. Make sure there are plenty of evergreen plants in the garden, though, to balance the effect.

- Vary the direction of the boards to create a range of effects. The boards will tend to lead the eye in the direction in which they point, so think carefully before you fix them in place. Lay them diagonally, widthways or lengthways, or mix two or more directions to separate different areas of the deck.

- A few cushion-forming plants around the edges of the deck will soften the effect and help it merge into its surroundings.

- Find a set of wooden furniture to match the deck and stain it in a contrasting colour. Alternatively, leave them both plain to create a more natural setting.

- A few containers of flowers or foliage will transform the deck into an appealing place to relax.

quick fix: from shady shrub border to woodland garden

Bark chippings and cocoa shell set off plants beautifully and can be used to enhance many different species. These materials look most at home in a shady border, underlying mixed shrubs and a few choice foliage plants, such as hostas and ferns. **care rating** ● ●

what's wrong with a shrub border?

There is nothing wrong with a well-structured shrub border that provides year-round colour, texture and structure. However, unless you choose your plants very carefully, shrub borders do require a certain amount of maintenance and shrubs that have been neglected and allowed to become overgrown produce smaller and fewer flowers or less reliable foliage colour and weeds will have gained a foothold.

Rather than prune the shrubs back hard, destroying the look of the border for a couple of years, you could transform your shady border to a woodland bed using a mulch of bark between some handsome shade-loving plants.

what's good about bark chippings?

Both bark chippings and cocoa shells suppress weeds by preventing light from reaching the soil beneath. For a really labour-free surface, however, lay thick plastic sheeting or a weed-suppressing membrane underneath and contain the material with a timber edging to hold it in place.

▲ *Cyclamen cilicium* planted in bark chippings adds colour to a woodland garden.

▶ Think about the way woodland plants grow in the wild when choosing plants: early spring flowers are followed by shade lovers as the tree canopy becomes thicker.

how it's done

1 Weed the border and carefully dig up any of the smaller plants that you want to keep. Wrap the rootballs in plastic bags and stand them in a shady corner out of the way. Leave the large plants in position and work round them.

2 Dig some well-rotted garden compost or other soil improver into the soil, rake it level and firm the soil with your feet.

3 Lay thick plastic or weed-suppressing membrane over the soil, cutting it to fit around any plants that are still in the border.

4 If necessary, put a log or timber edging in place to contain the bark chips and stop them spreading into other parts of the garden.

5 Cut cross-shaped holes in the plastic or membrane and plant a range of shade-loving plants through them.

6 Arrange a 5–8cm (2–3in) layer of bark chippings on top of the plastic or membrane to cover it completely.

plants for dry shade

Plant a selection of the following in your shady border for reliable year-round interest:

Alchemilla mollis (lady's mantle)

Asplenium scolopendrium (hart's tongue fern)

Aucuba japonica **'Crotonifolia'** (spotted laurel)

Berberis x stenophylla (barberry)

Bergenia cordifolia **'Purpurea'** (elephant's ears)

Brunnera macrophylla

Dryopteris filix-mas (male fern)

Elaeagnus pungens **'Maculata'**

Euonymus fortunei **'Emerald 'n' Gold'**

Geranium macrorrhizum

Hedera helix (common ivy)

Lamium maculatum **'White Nancy'** (deadnettle)

Polypodium vulgare (common polypody)

Pulmonaria officinalis (lungwort)

Vinca major **'Variegata'** (periwinkle)

quick fix: from rock garden to raised bed

Traditional rock gardens are among the most labour-intensive of all garden features. If you have moved into a house with a rock garden, your life will be much easier if you create instead a simple raised bed to allow easy access to the plants. **care rating** ●●●

what's wrong with a rock garden?

Not only is it tricky to reach all parts of a rock garden to tend the plants, but weeding between the rocks and plants is time-consuming and fiddly. Often rock gardens border a lawn and the grass grows up between the rocks where it is out of reach of the lawnmower and difficult to get at with edging shears. Unless you have a passion for true alpine species and are prepared to provide protection for plants that rot in excessive winter wet, the range of plants that are usually grown in a rock garden will grow equally happily in a well-constructed raised bed.

what's good about a raised bed?

Raised beds give easy access to the plants (and weeds) without uncomfortable bending over. This makes them a great idea for all of us, but especially for elderly or disabled gardeners who can tend the beds from a sitting position. The straight sides allow a mowing strip to be installed between the bed and the lawn, making cutting the grass much easier, too.

▼ Raised beds are suitable for all kinds of plants, from alpines to vegetables. They are easy to look after and so save time in comparison to more standard beds and borders.

how it's done

1 Lift any plants from the rock garden that are worth saving and wrap their rootballs in polythene bags while you make the raised bed. Dismantle the rock garden, saving the topsoil and some of the rocks.

2 Level the ground and stack up the railway sleepers to make the raised bed, alternating the rows at the corners to make the bed stronger. A depth of three sleepers is probably about right, but make it lower or higher if you like. Nail vertical bracing battens to the insides of the raised bed to hold the sleepers in place.

3 When the sleeper bed feels firm and secure put a good layer of drainage material in the bottom and then fill it with the saved soil. It is a good idea to incorporate some well-rotted garden compost or other organic matter, plus some fine grit to make an open, free-draining mixture. Firm the soil and top up again if necessary.

4 If you want to, arrange a few rocks in the soil to add interest, then plant up the bed with rock plants.

5 Mulch the surface of the soil with a 2.5cm (1in) layer of fine grit to retain moisture, suppress weeds and keep the necks of the plants dry.

small rock plants

grit as mulch over surface

large rocks

rock plants spilling over edges

railway sleepers in 3 rows

favourite plants for raised beds

Ajuga reptans **'Burgundy Glow'** (bugle)

Erigeron karvinskianus (fleabane)

Festuca glauca (blue fescue)

Galanthus nivalis (snowdrop)

Heuchera micrantha var. *diversifolia* **'Palace Purple'** (coral bells)

Imperata cylindrica **'Rubra'** (Japanese blood grass)

Nepeta x *faassenii* (catmint)

Saxifraga x *urbium* (London pride)

Sedum spectabile (ice plant)

Sempervivum cvs. (houseleek)

Stachys byzantina (lamb's ears)

Thymus serpyllum (thyme)

Tolmiea menziesii (pick-a-back plant)

▲ A mulch of bark chippings will help in a raised bed to prevent weeds growing between newly installed seasonal plants.

the shrub garden

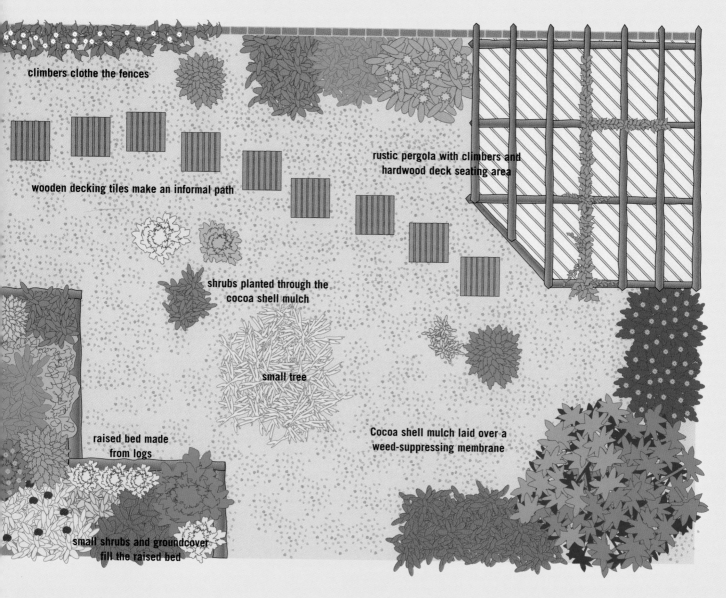

climbers clothe the fences

wooden decking tiles make an informal path

rustic pergola with climbers and
hardwood deck seating area

shrubs planted through the
cocoa shell mulch

small tree

Cocoa shell mulch laid over a
weed-suppressing membrane

raised bed made
from logs

small shrubs and groundcover
fill the raised bed

The shrub garden has a natural, rustic feel and makes use of sympathetic materials, including rustic poles, wooden decking and cocoa shell. The various elements it in are linked by the mulch of cocoa shell, which covers the ground. It is a layout that would be ideal for a garden in a rural setting but also for an urban one that is overlooked by nearby buildings as the pergola also provides privacy.

care rating ●

why this garden works

An area of decking under the pergola in the far corner of the garden provides a smart, stable seating area, and the rustic, climber-clad pergola casts the furniture into comfortable shade. Cocoa shell is used as a mulch to cover the floor of the garden, and provides a rich, chocolate scent as well as a soft, dry surface to walk on. The decking theme is extended to the square decking tiles, which form an informal stepping stone path down the garden. Handsome shrubs and small trees bring the garden to life, creating a tapestry of foliage colours and textures as well as seasonal flowers.

▶ A wooden pergola, or arbour, and decking are ideally suited to a garden that contains shrubs.

this is the garden for you if:

- You hate cutting the lawn
- You would like somewhere shady to sit and eat
- You like the enclosed, private feeling of being in a wood
- You want year-round colour and form from plants

care plan : the shrub garden

- Rake the cocoa shell mulch once a year to spread it evenly and top it up when necessary
- Collect fallen leaves from deciduous shrubs in autumn
- Prune flowering shrubs to improve flowering performance
- Cut back shrubs that become too large

◄ The witch hazel, *Hamamelis* x *intermedia* 'Jelena'.

top 20 plants

Aucuba japonica 'Crotonifolia' (spotted laurel)

Berberis x stenophylla (barberry)

Betula utilis var. jacquemontii (Himalayan birch)

Buddleja davidii (butterfly bush)

Chaenomeles x superba (flowering quince)

Clematis montana var. rubens 'Tetrarose'

Cotinus coggygria (smoke bush)

Crocus cvs.

Elaeagnus pungens 'Maculata'

Erica carnea (heather)

Hamamelis x intermedia (witch hazel)

Hedera helix (common ivy)

Ilex x altaclerensis 'Golden King' (holly)

Juniperus communis 'Compressa' (common juniper)

Mahonia japonica

Malus x zumi 'Golden Hornet' (crabapple)

Narcissus cvs. (daffodil)

Potentilla fruticosa (cinquefoil)

Prunus serrula (ornamental cherry/birch bark tree)

Vinca major 'Variegata' (periwinkle)

choosing plants

The shrubs have been chosen to provide different foliage colours for interest all year round. Although they are mostly evergreen, such as the aucuba and elaeagnus, deciduous shrubs provide seasonal interest and autumn colour, and plants such as the flowering quince and buddleia bloom at different times to extend the seasons of interest.

It is also important to selected a range of shrub shapes and forms. Unless it is clipped regularly, the cotinus will develop into a spreading, open shrub, while the erica forms a low, dense mound. One or two small trees provide height, and the ornamental cherry has been included because it also has interesting bark, which is a feature in winter.

The planting is finished with a few small bulbs, which will require no work at all but will provide a bright splash of colour in the dark days of early spring.

◄ The foliage and flowers of *Vinca major* 'Variegata'.

building a pergola and deck

A pergola, or arbour, is both useful and attractive: providing both somewhere secluded for you to sit and a framework for plants to climb over. Different materials can be used to suit any style, and rustic poles are particularly appropriate for an informal situation, such as this shrub garden. In this design, the pergola and low-level decking are constructed at the same time: although this may seem complex, it would in fact be far more complicated to build them separately.

1 Mark out the area with pegs and string and remove around 10cm (4in) of topsoil; make sure that the ground is level.

2 For each upright, dig a hole a further 70cm (28in) deep and set the post in compacted hardcore to 15cm (6in) below ground level. Fill the rest of the hole with concrete. Ensure that the posts are exactly vertical.

3 Line the area with weed-suppressing membrane.

4 Position bricks or concrete slabs to support the bearers 90cm (36in) apart at roughly 1.5m (5ft) intervals. Remember that the bearers should lie at right angles to the planks that will rest on them.

5 Lay the bearers on the bricks or slabs, and secure them to the end beams with galvanized brackets. To make the framework sturdy, fix cross-pieces between the bearers at 90cm (36in) intervals.

6 The planks are fixed to the bearers at right angles, with a pair of screws at each join to prevent the timber warping. Stagger the joins, and use an offcut 1cm (½in) wide to get an even space between the planks. Trim the plank ends and add a fascia board to conceal them if you wish.

7 Secure the top beams of the pergola and add cross-pieces to make it more sturdy.

8 Conceal the membrane underneath the decking with the same mulch used in the rest of the garden.

▲ Pergolas and decking whether left natural or painted, form an ideal combination with all sorts of plants.

the outdoor room

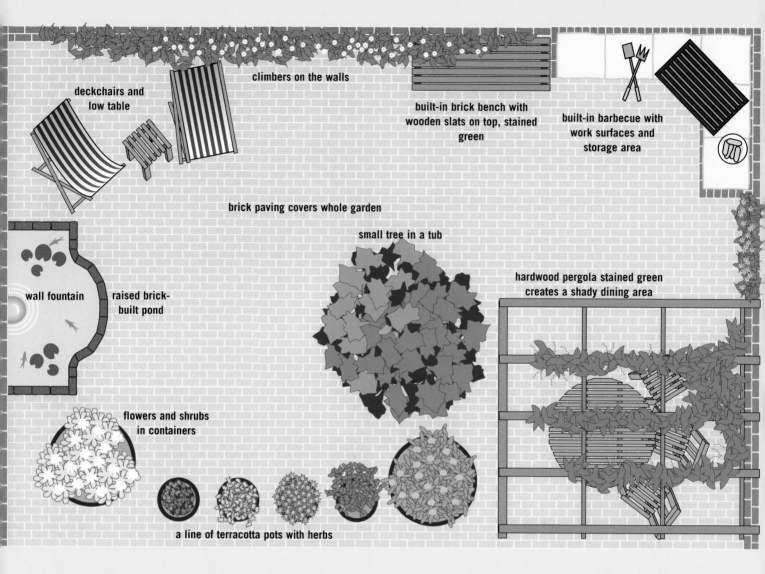

deckchairs and low table

climbers on the walls

built-in brick bench with wooden slats on top, stained green

built-in barbecue with work surfaces and storage area

brick paving covers whole garden

small tree in a tub

wall fountain

raised brick-built pond

hardwood pergola stained green creates a shady dining area

flowers and shrubs in containers

a line of terracotta pots with herbs

The outdoor room is designed to function as an extra room that extends the family's living space. It is the ideal solution for a busy family that has little time to spend working in the garden but that enjoys entertaining in a pleasant, relaxing atmosphere.

care rating ●

why this garden works

The whole garden is paved with handsome red bricks, attractive enough to be used over a large area, that provide a firm, all-weather surface. A hardwood pergola provides a shady dining area, while the deckchairs provide temporary seating for soaking up the sun. They are light enough to be moved easily, and because they can be folded they are ideal for storing out of the way in the garage in winter.

The small built-in barbecue is complete with work surfaces and storage space, making entertaining easy, and a raised pond and fountain add to the mood with soft gurgling noises. A few containers add seasonal colour, and leafy climbers clothe the walls. A line of terracotta pots provides growing space for a few herbs. The amount of care needed to maintain this garden depends on the plants chosen for the containers. If you choose permanent plants, the care is negligible; if you prefer seasonal bedding, you will need to replace it twice a year.

◀ Barbecues can be built in many different sizes to suit your needs. The metal parts can be bought in kit form, ready to fit into a brick surround.

▶ In a small outdoor room it is important to keep the space as uncluttered as possible.

this is the garden for you if:

- You enjoy eating outdoors with friends and family in summer
- You want a spacious, uncluttered area outdoors to provide extra living space
- You would like to grow herbs in containers to use on the barbecue
- You want a small water feature to provide the sound of splashing water

care plan : the outdoor room

- Remove some of the oxygenating plants if they choke the pond
- Clean the fountain head if it becomes blocked
- Water containers in warm weather
- Replace seasonal container plants twice a year, if necessary
- Sweep the paving from time to time

◄ Hydrangeas such as *H. macrophylla* 'Madame Emile Mouillère' are good for easy-care gardens as the flowers are long-lasting.

top 20 plants

Calendula officinalis (pot marigold)

Choisya ternata (Mexican orange blossom)

Clematis montana var. **rubens 'Tetrarose'**

Doronicum orientale (leopard's bane)

Euonymus fortunei 'Emerald 'n' Gold'

Humulus lupulus 'Aureus' (golden hop)

Hydrangea macrophylla

Laurus nobilis (bay)

Mentha spp. (mint)

Muscari armeniacum (grape hyacinth)

Origanum spp. (oregano)

Primula cvs. (primrose)

Rosmarinus officinalis (rosemary)

Salix caprea 'Kilmarnock' (Kilmarnock willow)

Santolina chamaecyparissus (cotton lavender)

Sorbus aria 'Lutescens' (whitebeam)

Thymus vulgaris (thyme)

Tulipa cvs. (tulip)

Viburnum plicatum 'Mariesii' (Japanese snowball bush)

Viola cvs. (pansy)

choosing plants

The aim in the outdoor room is to provide a selection of plants that will provide colour and interest, especially in summer when the garden is used for entertaining and enjoyment. Easy-care herbs, such as thyme, rosemary, bay and sage, which are evergreen and look good all year round, provide colour and aromatic foliage. A small tree in a tub adds height, and attractive flowering and foliage climbers clothe the walls as there are only a few plants in this garden. The containers can be filled with permanent elements, such as evergreens, and a few bulbs or bedding plants can be added to provide spring and summer colour if wished.

Oxygenating plants, such as *Hottonia palustris* (water violet), will keep the water clear in the pond, while a small waterlily floats on the surface to shade the water.

quick fixes for dull walls

Paint can have both a practical and an aesthetic role on a wall. For example, light-coloured paint can be used to brighten a dark wall in a shady corner, reflecting more light to the surrounding plants. It can also be used to hide ugly cement block or modern brick walls – dark green is useful because it creates a sympathetic backdrop to the garden. Brighter colours, such as blue or terracotta, can transform a patio garden, especially in town, and create a sunny ambience all year round.

Unappealing walls can be rendered with cement to give a flat surface with a granular texture. This creates a Mediterranean feel, and the wall can be painted in a complementary colour.

Mosaic can transform a wall and be an eye-catching decorative feature. Use broken pottery, tiles, shells or pebbles. Unless you are artistic, use a simple, geometric pattern for the best effect. Wall plaques or masks can also be used to add interest on a plain wall. They are often classical in design and are usually made from terracotta, cement or a stone substitute. They are especially effective when combined with climbing plants.

Wall pots and windowboxes can be attached to walls for a colourful display. However, cut down on the amount of watering needed as they will dry out quickly (see pages 94–7). Use a line of matching wall pots or a collection of various pots in a random pattern on the wall.

Climbing plants are an easy solution for a dull wall. Use self-clinging climbers or attach some supporting wires or trellis to the wall. Choose evergreen plants if you need to provide cover all year round. If the area in front of the wall is paved, plant the climbers in containers. Try growing two climbers together: one with year-round foliage and the other to provide seasonal flowers.

5 favourite climbers for walls

Instead of the clematis in this shrub garden, choose one of the following easy-care climbers:

- **Hedera spp.** (ivy), a self-clinging, evergreen climber, has glossy leaves, and many cultivars have bright variegation or interesting shapes.

- **Hydrangea anomala subsp. petiolaris** (climbing hydrangea) is a self-clinging, deciduous climber, which produces showy white flowers in summer.

- **Jasminum officinale** (common jasmine), a deciduous, twining climber, has fragrant white flowers in summer to autumn.

- **Parthenocissus quinquefolia** (Virginia creeper), a deciduous, self-clinging foliage climber, has striking autumn leaf colour.

- **Solanum crispum 'Glasnevin'** (potato vine) is a semi-evergreen, twining climber with purple flowers in summer, which does best grown against a warm wall.

▲ Ivy clothes part of a handsome wall which has been decorated with paint and a pattern of shells.

the jungle garden

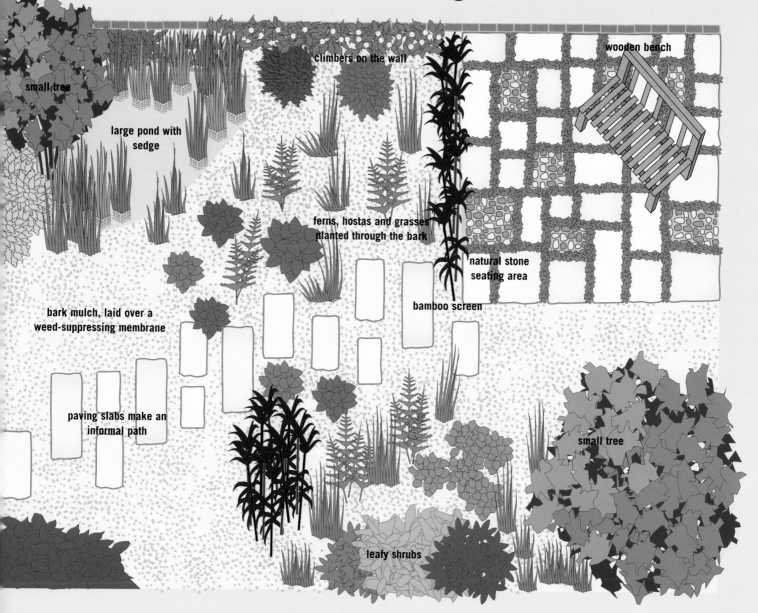

small tree

climbers on the wall

large pond with sedge

wooden bench

ferns, hostas and grasses planted through the bark

natural stone seating area

bark mulch, laid over a weed-suppressing membrane

bamboo screen

paving slabs make an informal path

small tree

leafy shrubs

In the jungle garden, the emphasis is on foliage plants that produce a rich tapestry of colours, textures and shapes. This is an ideal scheme for an urban garden, where the slightly exotic feeling is appropriate in the largely built-up surroundings.

care rating ●

why this garden works

Small, airy trees create dappled shade, where the soft light can play on the ferns, hostas, bamboos, grasses and shrubs beneath. The floor of the garden is covered with a bark mulch to complement the leafy plants that are planted through it. A firm seating area has been made from natural stone slabs. The slabs are of varying sizes, to add to the natural look of the garden, and they are interspersed with areas of cobbles to provide textural interest. The small carpeting plant *Soleirolia soleirolii* (baby's tears) has been allowed to grow in the gaps between the slabs and cobbles to make them more 'organic', and on one side of the garden a large pond, planted with sedges, adds to the jungle feel.

◀ *Acanthus spinosus* has enormous glossy leaves that create a jungle feel all year round. The towering flower spikes add drama in summer.

▶ Aim to include plants with many different leaf sizes and shapes to add variety.

this is the garden for you if:

- You like plenty of plants in your garden
- You want a green, shady place to relax
- You want a natural-looking space that will attract wildlife
- You want the interest provided by a well-planted pond

care plan : the jungle garden

- Cut back dead foliage of grasses, ferns and hostas in early spring (if not done in autumn)
- Remove over-vigorous carpeting plants, such as *Soleirolia soleirolii*, where they are not wanted from time to time
- Remove some of the pond plants if they become too vigorous
- Prune back unwanted shrub growth
- Rake over bark mulch once a year to spread evenly and top up if necessary

◄ *Asplenium scolopendrium* is a handsome evergreen fern.

top 20 plants

Acanthus spinosus (bear's breeches)
Ajuga reptans 'Burgundy Glow' (bugle)
Asplenium scolopendrium (hart's tongue fern)
Aucuba japonica 'Crotonifolia' (spotted laurel)
Betula utilis var. **jacquemontii** (Himalayan birch)
Carex elata 'Aurea' (Bowles' golden sedge)
Dryopteris filix-mas (male fern)
Epimedium grandiflorum (barrenwort)
Fatsia japonica (Japanese aralia)
Hakonechloa macra 'Aureola'
Hedera helix (common ivy)
Hosta sieboldiana var. **elegans**
Humulus lupulus 'Aureus' (golden hop)
Mahonia japonica
Miscanthus sinensis 'Zebrinus' (zebra grass)
Parthenocissus quinquefolia (Virginia creeper)
Phyllostachys nigra (black bamboo)
Polypodium vulgare (common polypody)
Sorbus aria 'Lutescens' (whitebeam)
Tolmiea menziesii (pick-a-back plant)

choosing plants

The plants in the jungle garden have been chosen for their foliage interest, and there is a wide range of different leaf shapes and sizes. Some shrubs, such as *Fatsia japonica* (Japanese aralia), have large, glossy leaves that make a strong impact. The plants are arranged close together to intensify the jungle feel.

Grasses are included to texture, colour and height, with some forming large clumps up to 2m (6ft) tall. The ferns and hostas provide leafy foliage at a lower level, and many ferns have an architectural, shuttlecock form that provides additional height and interest. A slow-growing bamboo creates a screen around the seating area. *Phyllostachys nigra* (black bamboo) is a handsome plant with black stems, and it does not spread as rapidly as some bamboos.

Oxygenating plants keep the pond water clear, and reed-like plants, such as *Typha minima* (dwarf reedmace), could be added to provide extra height and cover for visiting birds and wildlife.

laying bark mulch

Bark mulch makes an ideal surface for a jungle garden because it is more sympathetic to the plants themselves than gravel would be. Like cocoa shell mulch, it is also very child friendly. Whether you are making a new garden or adapting an existing border, follow the steps below.

1 Lift the smaller plants out of the border, keeping intact the rootballs of those plants you want to retain, and set them aside in a shady position. If you plan to leave them for some time or if the weather is warm wrap the rootballs in plastic bags and keep them moist. Leave large plants in the border and work around them.

2 Weed the border, removing the roots of perennial weeds. Rake the soil level and compact it lightly with your feet.

3 Lay a sheet of heavy-duty polythene or weed-suppressing membrane over the bare soil. Cut it to fit closely around existing plants and avoid leaving any gaps between sheets. Overlap pieces of sheet if necessary.

4 Return the kept plants and add new ones to the border by cutting cross-shaped holes in the membrane and planting the plants through them. For a jungle garden, you can plant quite densely. Water the plants well.

5 Arrange a 5cm (2in) layer of bark mulch over the whole border to cover the plastic or membrane. Rake it level.

6 Edge the mulch, using a sympathetic material such as log roll or strips of treated timber.

▶ The idea of a jungle garden is to create the impression of lush foliage while not, in fact, letting the plants take over.

the stone and gravel garden

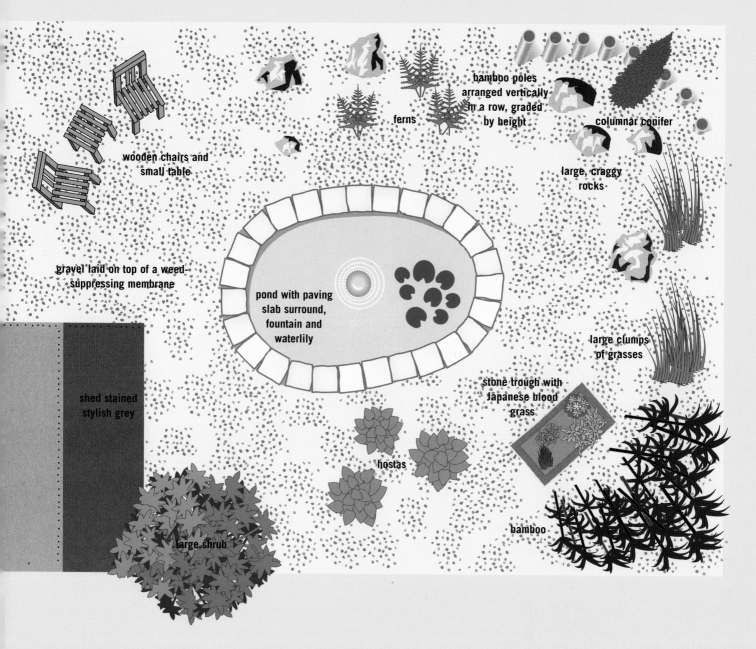

bamboo poles
arranged vertically
in a row, graded
by height

ferns

columnar conifer

wooden chairs and
small table

large, craggy
rocks

gravel laid on top of a weed-
suppressing membrane

pond with paving
slab surround,
fountain and
waterlily

large clumps
of grasses

stone trough with
Japanese blood
grass

shed stained
stylish grey

hostas

large shrub

bamboo

This oriental-style garden is relatively minimalist, with just a few strong elements making up the design. It is an ideal scheme for a garden surrounded by walls and buildings, but the style is also suitable for a garden that has views beyond its own boundaries, when the idea of the 'borrowed landscape' can be used.

care rating ●

why this garden works

The main emphasis is a large, oval pond in the centre of the garden, which has a fountain and, at the other end of the pond, away from the turbulence, a waterlily. The garden floor is covered with grey-brown gravel, and large, craggy rocks act as focal points to off set carefully placed ferns, grasses and bamboos.

In one corner, a gracefully curving row of thick bamboo poles of varying sizes emphasizes the oriental theme and adds year-round height and interest to the garden. The garden shed has been stained in a charcoal grey to enhance the minimalist scheme, making it a stylish feature.

▲ *Miscanthus sinensis* 'Zebrinus' forms a tall upright clump of stripy leaves. The feathery plumes appear in late summer.

◄ Introduce a few simple stone sculptures into the garden for added oriental atmosphere.

this is the garden for you if:

- You want somewhere calming and soothing to relax in peace and quiet
- You like the sound of water splashing from a fountain
- You like a graphic, minimalist look
- You want a really low-maintenance garden

care plan : the stone and gravel garden

- Rake the gravel from time to time to spread it evenly and top it up if necessary
- Remove dead leaves from hostas, ferns and grasses in early spring (if not done in autumn)
- Remove some of the oxygenating plants from the pond if it becomes choked with vegetation

◄ The dramatic foliage and flowers of *Fatsia japonica*.

top 10 plants

Asplenium scolopendrium (hart's tongue fern)

Dryopteris filix-mas (male fern)

Fatsia japonica (Japanese aralia)

Hakonechloa macra 'Aureola'

Hedera helix (common ivy)

Hosta sieboldiana var. **elegans**

Imperata cylindrica 'Rubra' (Japanese blood grass)

Juniperus communis 'Compressa' (common juniper)

Miscanthus sinensis 'Zebrinus' (zebra grass)

Phyllostachys nigra (black bamboo)

choosing plants

This garden contains only a limited number of plants, relying instead on large rocks and bamboo poles for structure. Those plants included must really earn their place and are largely selected for their architectural effect. Tall, arching ferns and hostas have elegant fronds and leaves in summer, while the columnar conifer provides year-round structure and foliage colour. The *Fatsia japonica* (Japanese aralia) has been selected for its large, striking foliage and for its architectural qualities.

The slow-growing bamboo can be easily kept under control, and the *Imperata cylindrica* 'Rubra' (Japanese blood grass) brings some welcome colour for the summer months. The trough in which it is growing will add shape for winter when the grass dies down.

Oxygenating plants in the pond keep the water clear, while a waterlily adds surface interest.

edging options for gravel

To stop gravel spreading to adjoining areas of the garden you will need to edge it. There is a wide choice of suitable materials, provided that the minimalist theme is retained. Set bricks, paving slabs, stone setts or pressure-treated timber so that they protrude a few centimetres above the gravel. Use only one type of edging.

For a classic look, use edging tiles around the gravel garden. Or, for a more modern feel, cut a strip of lead sheet, about 20cm (8in) deep, to fit around the edges of the gravel garden. Insert the bottom 10cm (4in) into the soil and cut the top of the lead into a simple pattern.

Alternatively, contain the gravel with strips of pressure-treated timber 2.5cm (1in) wide. Use 12.5cm (5in) planks and set them into the ground so that they protrude by about 5cm (2in) above the gravel.

For a real oriental look, use a row of giant bamboo canes, cobbles set in concrete or larger boulders.

statues and ornaments

A small number of carefully placed ornaments can be a welcome addition to a minimalist garden, creating focal points and providing character. In the minimalist garden less is more.

There is no need to spend large sums of money: an old rock or a piece of gnarled driftwood can be just as effective as an expensive mock Japanese lantern.

Equally, there is no need to stick to an oriental theme: simple geometric objects such as stone spheres or pyramids can be very effective. Stone balls of different sizes can work really well if grouped in threes or fives.

▼ Gravel, large rocks, bamboo canes and cobbles combine well together to create a varied and interesting scheme. Few plants are needed to complete the effect.

the simple garden

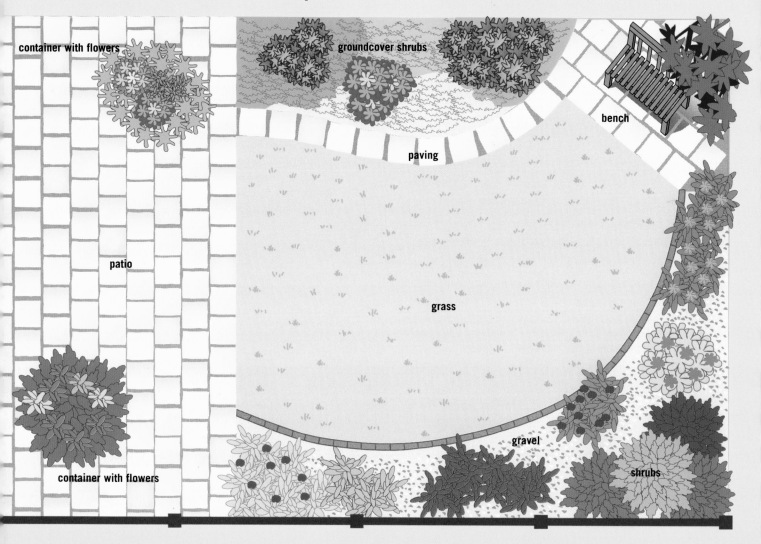

container with flowers

groundcover shrubs

bench

paving

patio

grass

container with flowers

gravel

shrubs

The garden has a number of basic elements – patio, lawn and borders – that have been combined to create a simple, easy-care garden. It is the sort of garden that can work almost anywhere, and the combination of hard surfaces and planting is appropriate for urban, suburban and country gardens alike.

care rating ●

why it works

The large paved patio next to the house provides plenty of space for a dining table and chairs or for sunloungers, and it can brightened with colourful containers or even easy herbs or vegetables.

A path of paving slabs joins the patio to a small seating area, sited under the shade of the existing tree at the bottom of the garden. On one side of the garden an area of shrubs and groundcover plants provides foliage and flowers but requires the minimum of care, while on the other side a small gravel garden provides space for a few more shrubs and some reliable, colourful perennials.

The gentle curve of the lawn unifies the separate elements of the garden, drawing the eye towards the focal point of the bench at the far end. Because the lawn is curved, the garden appears wider and less 'boxy'. It is also a good contrast with the hard edge of the patio and its more formal, geometric paving. The lawn is edged on all sides by hard surfaces, set slightly below the level of the grass. This makes mowing easy and eliminates the need for time-consuming edging; it also prevent plants from the borders flopping over on to the grass, making mowing more difficult and causing bald patches in the grass.

▲ Although containers do require regular watering, large pots take longer to dry out than small ones. Grouping them also makes watering less time consuming.

this is the garden for you if:

- You need a lawn for the children to play on
- You want year-round colour, texture and structure from your plants
- You do not want to spend time weeding
- You enjoy relaxing and entertaining on the patio
- You value a quiet, private corner

care plan : the simple garden

- Mow the lawn once a week in summer
- Replant containers with flowers as necessary
- Prune flowering shrubs to improve flowering performance
- Cut back herbaceous perennials when the foliage dies back or in spring
- Feed shrubs and flowers
- Weed and feed the lawn occasionally
- Remove fallen leaves from the garden in autumn

◄ *Geranium macrorrhizum* is a tough perennial.

top 20 plants

Anthemis punctata subsp. *cupaniana*

Crataegus laevigata 'Paul's Scarlet' (hawthorn)

Dicentra spectabilis (bleeding heart)

Euonymus fortunei 'Emerald Gaiety'

Geranium macrorrhizum (cranesbill)

Hedera spp. (ivy)

Hemerocallis (daylily)

Hypericum calycinum (rose of Sharon)

Ilex x altaclerensis 'Golden King' (holly)

Jasminum nudiflorum (winter jasmine)

Lavatera 'Barnsley' (mallow)

Nepeta x faassenii (catmint)

Pelargonium

Potentilla fruticosa (shrubby cinquefoil)

Ribes sanguineum (flowering currant)

Rudbeckia fulgida var. sullivantii 'Goldsturm' (coneflower)

Solidago (golden rod)

Stachys byzantina (lamb's ears)

Vinca major 'Variegata' (periwinkle)

Viola Ultima Mixed (winter-flowering pansy)

choosing plants

The aim is to choose plants that are easy to care for and that provide value for the space they take up. Any of the plants listed in the top twenty plants section would be suitable in this type of garden.

Make sure that there are some evergreen plants to provide a backdrop and structure in winter, and cultivars with variegated foliage, such as the euonymus, earn their keep all year round. Introduce variations in height, too, because gardens on a single level rarely look interesting. Here, for example, the tall spires of solidago will tower above the catmint. Plant the perennials in clumps of three or five of each type so that they have maximum impact; interspersing different plants can look messy and bitty.

Groundcover plants are valued for their weed-suppressing capability, but they can also be used for texture and colour. Variegated ivy is easy to control – clip the leaves in spring or remove entire stems if they wander too far – and the periwinkle bears violet-blue flowers above its mat of variegated foliage.

Make sure you have some colour in the garden in each of the seasons. The jasmine's pretty yellow flowers appear in winter, while the geranium will brighten the border from early summer onwards.

style solutions for paving

Bricks and pavers are available in a variety of colours and many different effects can be created by mixing them. Pavers are rather regimented and regular in appearance, so use them in more modern settings. House bricks are softer in colour and irregular in size. Make sure the bricks or pavers are frostproof before you lay them, and remember that house bricks aren't always frostproof on all surfaces. Bricks can become slippery when damp, especially in shady places; if necessary, scrub them with algicide from time to time. Lay bricks and pavers on sand, over a firm hardcore base.

Real stone slabs, such as York stone, are by far the most beautiful of the available paving slabs, but they are also by far the most expensive. Imitation stone is also now widely available and varies from realistic to unattractive. Those with textured surfaces are the best, so choose carefully.

Concrete paving slabs are more regular in appearance than real stone, and they usually have a perfectly flat surface, which makes them ideal for patios. They come in a variety of colours, of which the natural tones generally look most sympathetic in the garden. Artificial colours suit a modern environment but they can look gaudy and garish. Broken slabs or irregular shapes can be used for crazy paving. Square or rectangular slabs, laid in a regular pattern, are suited to many more situations, so think carefully before you decide. A patio should last a lifetime, so make sure you will be happy with it whatever else you decide to do with the garden. Lay slabs on a sand base over a layer of well-compacted hardcore.

Setts are small, square, stone blocks, usually made from granite. They are fiddly to lay but make handsome paths, edgings or infills between paving slabs. Their uneven surface makes them look natural and sympathetic in many settings, and the small, square setts can be used to create curves or other flowing patterns. They are hard-wearing but rather expensive.

▶ In a small area, it is best to keep any paving material simple. Here, the bricks lead the eye to the bench but do not distract from the planting.

the wild garden

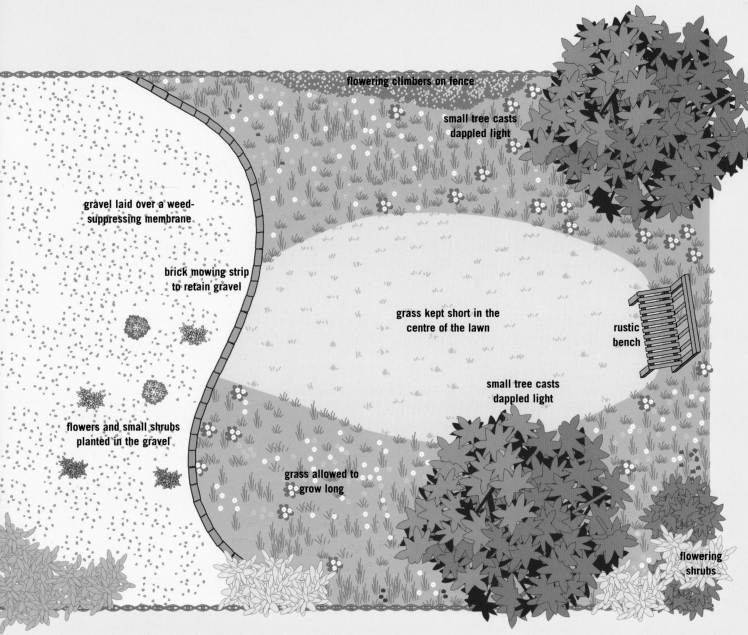

flowering climbers on fence

small tree casts
dappled light

gravel laid over a weed-
suppressing membrane

brick mowing strip
to retain gravel

grass kept short in the
centre of the lawn

rustic
bench

small tree casts
dappled light

flowers and small shrubs
planted in the gravel

grass allowed to
grow long

flowering
shrubs

The wild style is perfect for a rural garden, but it can also offer a quiet retreat in town, making you feel close to nature. The intimate nature of this pleasant, enclosed garden is emphasized by the willow hurdles, which enclose it on both sides.

care rating ●

why this garden works

Although there is a fairly large proportion of lawn in terms of the overall space, mowing is kept to a minimum by allowing most of the grass to grow long. The long grass is cut twice a year, once in early spring and once in late summer, and this regime should encourage some wild flowers, such as buttercups and daisies, to grow in the grass to provide colour and attract insects. The grass in the centre of the garden is kept short to allow access to the bench and provide a space for having picnics.

This garden has an area of gravel next to the house to provide space for a table and chairs, and a few shrubs and smaller plants grow through the gravel to soften the effect.

The curved line of red bricks, separating the areas of gravel and grass, serves the dual purpose of providing a mowing edge to eliminate the need to clip the grass edges after mowing and of softening the break between the two surfaces. A straight line would have emphasized the squareness of the garden.

The planting incorporates two established trees, which provide pleasant shade at the far end of the garden where a simple wooden bench is positioned. To lessen the shadows cast by the trees it might be necessary to raise the crowns a little to allow more light to reach the lawn, which will not do well in shade.

▲ *Buddleja davidii* is a wonderful plant for a wild garden: as well as bearing flowers, it will attract and feed a range of colourful butterflies and other insects such as honeybees.

this is the garden for you if:

- You want a relaxed, informal garden with a natural look
- You want to encourage wildlife to visit your garden
- You would like a range of interesting plants

care plan : the wild garden

- Mow the centre of the lawn every two weeks in summer
- Mow the long grass twice a year, cutting it to no less than 8cm (3in) long
- Remove unwanted weeds from the long grass, such as stinging nettles and brambles, twice a year
- Prune flowering shrubs to improve flowering performance
- Rake gravel from time to time to spread it evenly and top it up from time to time

◀ The mahogany bark of *Prunus serrula*.

top 20 plants

Alchemilla mollis (lady's mantle)

Berberis thunbergii (barberry)

Betula utilis var. *jacquemontii* (Himalayan birch)

Buddleja davidii (butterfly bush)

Clematis montana var. *rubens* 'Tetrarose'

Crataegus laevigata 'Paul's Scarlet' (hawthorn)

Dipsacus fullonum (teasel)

Geranium macrorrhizum

Hedera helix (common ivy)

Lamium maculatum 'White Nancy' (deadnettle)

Lavandula angustifolia 'Hidcote' (lavender)

Lavatera 'Barnsley' (mallow)

Lonicera periclymenum (honeysuckle)

Malus x *zumi* 'Golden Hornet' (crabapple)

Narcissus cvs. (daffodil)

Potentilla fruticosa (cinquefoil)

Prunus serrula (birch bark tree)

Sorbus aucuparia (mountain ash)

Tiarella cordifolia (foam flower)

Viburnum plicatum 'Mariesii' (Japanese snowball bush)

choosing plants

The plants in the wild garden are chosen because they have a pretty, natural look. *Alchemilla mollis*, for example, produces frothy sprays of tiny yellow-green flowers above its neat mounds of leaves, and the *Lamium maculatum* (deadnettle) spreads, forming a delightful silvery carpet. One or two small trees, such as the reliable *Malus* x *zumi* 'Golden Hornet' (crabapple) and *Betula utilis* var. *jacquemontii* (Himalayan birch), will cast a pleasant dappled shade. If you can, sow a grass seed mixture that is specially designed for shade so the lawn will thrive.

A few flowering shrubs will provide structure and seasonal colour, from the spring colour of the daffodil to the late summer blooms of the buddleja. Small, cushion-forming plants have been selected for the gravel area, while flowering climbers, such as the fragrant honeysuckle, frame the garden with soft foliage and flowers.

why choose gravel?

Gravel is one of the most useful and flexible materials available to gardeners. It helps to keep the soil moist, cutting down on watering and if laid over a membrane or plastic sheet will eliminate the need to weed, water or mulch.

1 Lift smaller plants, keeping the rootballs intact, and set them aside in a shady position. If you plan to leave them for some time or if the weather is warm wrap the rootballs in plastic bags and keep them moist. Work around large plants.

2 Weed the border, removing the roots of perennial weeds, rake the soil level and compact it lightly with your feet.

3 Lay a sheet of heavy-duty polythene or weed-suppressing membrane over the bare soil. Cut it to fit closely around existing plants and avoid leaving any gaps between sheets.

4 Return the plants to the border by cutting cross-shaped holes in the plastic of membrane and planting the plants through the holes. Water the plants well.

5 Edge the border using one of the suggestions on page 67 and arrange a 2–3cm (1in) layer of gravel over the border.

low-mow meadow lawns

An easy-care alternative to having to mow the grass regularly is to allow some of it to grow into a meadow lawn. Long grass can look attractive and brings a wild, natural look even to a town garden. If you don't want to go all the way, regularly mow a small area close to the house for sitting out and let the rest of the grass, farther from the house, grow longer. This approach is particularly appropriate for areas that are hard to mow, such as slopes and banks.

Try to encourage a few wildflowers to grow in the grass – it won't be a true wildflower meadow without some expert care, but it will look pretty nonetheless, especially if you plant some *Narcissus* (daffodil) bulbs in it for a cheerful spring display. Cut the meadow once in early spring and again in late summer, no shorter than about 8cm (3in). Pull up unwanted weeds, such as brambles and stinging nettles, as soon as you see them to stop them taking over.

▲ Gravel makes a good foil for many plants, especially those with silver foliage which seems to be enhanced particularly well.
◄ *Alchemilla mollis* has a soft, natural look that makes it perfect for an informal setting.

plant it

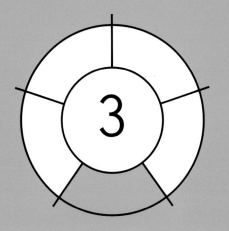

No garden, even the most minimalist, would be complete without a few plants, but there is no escaping the fact that in every garden it is the plants that require the most attention. However, it is possible to plan and adapt your beds and borders to cut down on unnecessary weeding, watering and plant care, so that you have the time to enjoy the beauty and benefits of a few colourful plants and even some tasty, home-grown herbs and vegetables.

One of the most important aspects of making beds and borders easier to care for is to choose plants that will be naturally happy in the conditions you have to offer. Pick shade-loving plants for shady places, sun-lovers for sunny places and take the quality of the soil into consideration: there is no point trying to grow a Mediterranean plant, such as *Rosmarinus officinalis* (rosemary), in a moist border, for

example. You will be disappointed when the plant refuses to grow, and you will have the frustration of having to replace it, even if it manages to survive for a couple of years. If you choose the right subjects for their positions in the garden, your plants should remain healthy, resist diseases, grow bushy and compact and save you lots of work later on.

Although half the battle is to choose plants that are suited to your borders, some plants are simply easier to look after than others. Select plants that are naturally resistant to diseases, don't require complicated pruning or constant cutting back or deadheading, are resistant to drought and will be happy to be left alone for a number of years without any fuss. Included in this chapter are some easy planting schemes, using the easy-care plants listed on pages 140–47, and you can follow these or adapt them to suit your own garden. All you need to do is sit back and enjoy them.

'if you choose the right subjects for their positions in the garden, your plants should remain healthy, resist diseases, grow bushy and compact and save you lots of work later on'

◄ Annual flowers, such as poppies and cornflowers, can be sown straight into the soil to fill gaps in beds and borders between other plants.

▲ When choosing plants for an easy-care garden go for those that suit your soil type and climate: they will thrive much better and need far less maintenance.

◄ The best way to prevent weeds growing is not to allow them any room. Dense planting of perennials, such as *Lavandula angustifolia* 'Hidcote', prevents weeds from gaining a foothold.

effortless borders

When it comes to planting up your borders, the golden rules are to choose the right easy-care plant for the right place, to provide the conditions for it to grow healthily and to prevent weeds that will deprive the plant of moisture and nutrients growing around it.

what type of soil do you have?

The type of soil you have will affect the types of plants that will do well in your garden. Take a handful of moist soil and you will be able to see whether it is clay, sand or in-between. Clay soil will form a heavy, flexible ball, which can be moulded without breaking. Sandy soil feels gritty and the ball will crumble if you squeeze it lightly. If you are lucky, your soil will be somewhere between these extremes, what is called a loam soil. If you have clay or sandy soil dig in plenty of well-rotted organic matter, such as leaf mould, garden compost or manure, before planting. Even with this treatment, be sure to choose plants that will enjoy the conditions on offer, whether it is heavy, moist clay or light, free-draining sandy soil.

   You should also know if your soil is acid or alkaline because this will also affect the plants that do well. Buy an inexpensive soil-testing kit from a garden centre and follow the instructions. Test soil from several parts of your garden, because it can vary within even fairly limited areas. If the soil is neutral, mildly acidic or mildly alkaline, any of the plants listed on pages 140–47 will thrive. If, however, it is strongly acid or alkaline, you will need to check with the nursery before buying a plant. There's no point in trying to make a plant grow in a soil that is unsuitable for it. It will never grow well, and you will eventually have to replace it.

▲ All of these plants require free-draining soil and would soon die in moist conditions. The gravel and paving stones create an arid feel to the design that complements the plants well.

is your garden in sun or shade?

The amount of sun or shade a border gets also affects the plants that you will be able to grow there. Shade-loving plants will scorch and wither in hot sun, while sun-loving plants will become leggy and shy to flower in a shady position. Pick the right plants for more attractive and less demanding flowerbeds.

are your plants under threat from children and animals?

If you have active children or dogs playing in the garden it is best to choose tough plants that will survive a bit of trampling or a fast-moving football. Avoid plants with brittle stems, those with soft, fleshy growth and small plants that will disappear altogether. If you are really concerned and would like to protect your plants, consider erecting a low fence around your borders to save them from the worst effects of trampling feet and exuberant dogs.

golden rules for low-maintenance borders

In addition to selecting the right plants for the garden, there are ways to make your borders easier to look after. Take a few simple measures and your flowerbeds will all but take care of themselves:

- Keep borders small
- Edge borders
- Plant close

Keeping borders small will cut down on the labour involved. Reduce the overall area of planting and increase the hard surfaces, but make sure that the borders you do have are positioned for maximum impact, placing them where they can be appreciated from many different viewpoints to give the feeling of there being more plants than there actually are. Long, narrow borders are the easiest to tend, because you can reach all of the plants without stepping on the soil, as this would compact it and increase the need for digging. An alternative is to lay a few paving slabs in the border to act as stepping stones.

Border edgings, such as bricks, wooden planks or edging tiles, will help to retain the soil and mulch in a border and keep it from spilling on to adjacent paths and paving. Where a border is adjacent to a lawn, incorporate a mowing strip into your choice of edging as trimming lawn edges is a tedious and unnecessary job (see pages 132–3).

When you are planting, place the flowering and foliage plants reasonably close together so that they soon grow to cover the soil and stop weeds growing. This arrangement also allows the plants to support each other so there is no need to stake taller perennials. The principle works if you are planting a number of different plants in a border or if you are planting a large group of the same plant. However, take care that you do not plant so closely that the mature border will look cramped and overcrowded.

▲ This border has a decorative edging and a mowing strip, combining aesthetics and practicality.

the best start

To give plants the best possible start so that they will grow healthily without help and soon fill out to cover the bare soil:

- Improve the soil before planting
- Choose the right site for each plant, in terms of soil type and sun and shade
- Water well after planting
- Feed regularly for maximum vigour

year-round colour

Some plants offer colour and interest in every season, and these are especially important in gardens with limited planting, where every plant has to earn its keep. It is not just flowers that provide seasonal colour: there are plants with decorative berries in autumn, beautiful bark that shows up best in winter or handsome variegated foliage that is bright and exciting all year round.

In addition to individual star performers, plant for year-round effect by using different plants in association with each other. One may provide striking spring flowers, another summer berries, another autumn colour and another evergreen foliage, so the overall display has something of interest whatever the season.

Remember, too, that you can introduce colour and interest by means other than plants. Brightly stained fences and decking can add strong colours, even in the depths of winter, and statues and other ornaments can grace a patio whatever the season.

▲ The evergreen foliage of *Elaeagnus pungens* 'Maculata' creates a bright splash of colour in the garden all year round.

calendar of colour

spring	summer	autumn	winter
Bulbs such as crocuses, daffodils and *Muscari armeniacum* (grape hyacinth)	Bedding flowers, such as *Eschscholzia*, *Nigella* and pelargoniums	Coloured foliage on deciduous trees and shrubs	Colourful tree bark on *Prunus* and *Betula*
Early perennials such as *Doronicum orientale*, brunneras and *Dicentra spectabilis*	Perennials, such as *Nepeta*, *Hemerocallis* and *Crocosmia*	Late perennials, such as *Solidago* and echinaceas	Winter-flowering bulbs
Flowering shrubs, such as *Berberis*, *Ribes* and *Viburnum plicatum*	Flowering shrubs, such as buddlejas, hydrangeas and lavender	Ornamental grass seedheads	Foliage on evergreen perennials, such as some forms of *Pulmonaria*, *Saxifraga* x *urbium* and sempervivums
Tree blossom on *Malus* and *Prunus*	Summer bulbs, such as *Allium*	Fruits on shrubs and trees, such as *Malus*, cotoneasters, *Pyracantha*, *Chaenomeles* and holly	Dried heads of grasses still on the plants
Unfurling fern fronds	Foliage plants, such as ornamental grasses and hostas	Rose hips	Drying heads of *Sedum spectabile* and other perennials
Catkins on trees such as *Corylus* and *Salix*	Evergreen foliage	Evergreen foliage	Flowering shrubs, such as *Jasminum nudiflorum*, *Hamamelis* spp. and mahonias
Evergreen foliage, such as *Santolina*, elaeagnus, *Ilex*, *Fatsia japonica* and juniper			Evergreen foliage
			Winter bedding, such as pansies and primroses

evergreens

All trees and shrubs provide structure and year-round effect in a border, but evergreens provide colour in winter in the form of handsome foliage, some bright and variegated. Choose slow-growing forms that won't need cutting so soon if they outgrow the space available. Most evergreen shrubs, including conifers, don't require cutting back or pruning.

For a border that will look after itself, plant a varied selection of evergreen shrubs, mixing tall, upright plants with low, dumpy ones, and green foliage with blue, yellow, bronze or variegated. Try to include at least some shrubs that have flowers to provide seasonal variation. Evergreens are also the best plants for suppressing weeds as they are the most efficient at preventing light from reaching the soil beneath.

▲ This evergreen display combines a variety of foliage colours and textures, as well as overall plant forms and sizes to make a varied border that will give interest all year.

plants for year-round effect **e** = evergreen **d** = deciduous

plant	spring	summer	autumn	winter
Ajuga reptans 'Burgundy Glow' (bugle) **e**	Blue flowers	Blue flowers	Purple foliage	Purple foliage
Aucuba japonica 'Crotonifolia' (spotted laurel) **e**	Small red flowers	Variegated foliage	Red berries	Variegated foliage
Berberis stenophylla (barberry) **e**	Yellow flowers	Glossy foliage	Blue berries	Glossy foliage
Bergenia cordifolia 'Purpurea' (elephant's ears) **e**	Pink flowers	Red-tinged foliage	Red-tinged foliage	Pink flowers
Betula utilis var. *jacquemontii* (Himalayan birch) **d**	Catkins	Bright green foliage	Yellow foliage	White bark
Elaeagnus pungens 'Maculata' **e**	Variegated foliage	Variegated foliage	White flowers	Red berries
Fatsia japonica (Japanese aralia) **e**	Large, glossy foliage	Large, glossy foliage	Cream flowers	Black fruits
Hakonechloa macra 'Aureola' **d**	Stripy foliage	Seedheads	Red-flushed foliage	Rustling brown stems
Hamamelis x *intermedia* (witch hazel) **d**	Foliage	Foliage	Red-yellow foliage	Fragrant yellow flowers
Hedera helix (common ivy) **e**	Glossy foliage	Glossy foliage	White-green flowers	Black berries
Ilex x *altaclerensis* 'Golden King' (holly) **e**	White flowers	Variegated foliage	Red berries	Variegated foliage
Mahonia japonica **e**	Blue fruits	Architectural foliage	Architectural foliage	Yellow flowers
Prunus serrula (birch bark tree) **d**	White blossom	Red, cherry-like fruits	Yellow foliage	Glossy, coppery bark
Sedum spectabile (ice plant) **d**	Fleshy foliage	Pink flowers	Pink flowers	Brown flowerheads

using groundcover

One of the least arduous ways to plant a border is to use spreading plants, which soon grow together to cover the soil and prevent weeds from growing. There are many attractive plants that can be used and groundcover certainly need not be a dreary option. Although low, spreading plants are the most common for groundcover, taller plants are also suitable, so an area of groundcover doesn't have to consist of flat, featureless planting.

The easy-care gardener will include a good selection of groundcover plants in beds and borders. These useful plants act in much the same way as a mulch of gravel or bark chippings by carpeting the soil so that annual weeds cannot colonize bare ground. They therefore help to minimize the amount of work involved in keeping the border tidy.

Any plants that produce plenty of foliage can be used as groundcover as long as they are planted close enough together to exclude light from the ground.

Remember that, although groundcover plants will reduce the amount of weeding you will have to do, they will not stop perennial weeds that are already present in the soil growing up through them. When you are preparing the ground for planting, it is important to remove all perennial weed roots. Moreover, when you first put the plants you are using as groundcover in the ground you must apply a mulch over the bare soil or weeds will simply colonize the ground that you have so carefully prepared. Bark chippings are ideal for the purpose. Lay them to a depth of at least 5cm (2in).

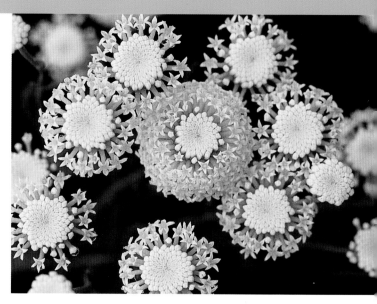

▲ *Santolina chamaecyparissus* 'Lemon Queen' has silvery foliage covered with button-like flowers in summer. Grow it in well-drained soil in a sunny site.

successful groundcover

- Clear the ground of all weeds before planting and add lots of well-rotted organic matter to get the groundcover plants off to a good start.

- Choose the right plants for the situation, taking into account soil type, sun and shade.

- Choose relatively fast-growing plants, which will soon cover the soil.

- If the plants spread by the growth of horizontal stems, cover the soil with black polythene or a weed-suppressing membrane and lay bark or gravel on top to suppress the weeds while the plants are filling out.

- If the plants spread by creeping roots, mulch the soil with organic matter to prevent weeds getting a good hold before the groundcover plants cover the soil. You may have to weed the border for a year or so before the groundcover is effective, but you will have years of no weeding to look forward to at the end of it.

◄ Pulmonarias make handsome groundcover in shady areas, with their silver-spotted leaves and blue, white or red flowers.

15 best groundcover plants

Acanthus spinosus (bear's breeches

Ajuga reptans **'Burgundy Glow'** (bugle)

Anthemis punctata subsp. *cupaniana*

Bergenia cordifolia **'Purpurea'** (elephant's ears)

Brunnera macrophylla

Epimedium grandiflorum (barrenwort)

Geranium macrorrhizum

Hedera spp. (ivy)

Heuchera micrantha var. *diversifolia* **'Palace Purple'** (coral bells)

Hypericum calycinum (rose of Sharon)

Lamium maculatum **'White Nancy'** (deadnettle)

Pulmonaria officinalis (lungwort)

Santolina chamaecyparissus (cotton lavender)

Saxifraga x *urbium* (London pride)

Vinca major **'Variegata'** (periwinkle)

choosing a mulch

Material	Pros	Cons
black polythene	Cheap, widely available and effective	Unsightly
bark chippings	Looks natural in almost every garden	Larger chippings can be unattractive
farmyard manure	Good soil conditioner	Must not be used fresh May contain weed seeds
grass clippings	Readily available Suitable for the back of the border	Unattractive Should not be used in deep layers
gravel	Attractive Widely available	Not suitable for all borders, it tends to get mixed into the ground unless laid over a membrane; it needs regular topping up and will 'travel' to neighbouring lawns and paths
leaf mould	Looks natural; a good soil conditioner	Not easy to obtain unless home-made
mushroom compost	Good soil conditioner	It must not be used fresh and contains chalk so should not be used near acid-loving plants

◄ Bergenias have large, glossy leaves, often tinged with red or purple. They will survive in just about any conditions and produce showy pink flowers in late winter and spring.

plants for problem areas

Almost every garden has one or more areas that present problems, where it is not obvious what treatment is suitable and which plants will thrive. There is always something that can be done, however, so treat them more as challenges and follow the advice below to tackle them.

shade

Choosing plants for deep shade is never easy, and under a large tree there is often the additional problem of impoverished, dry soil as the tree's roots search for moisture and nutrients. It will be almost impossible to get grass to grow in such conditions. There are two possible solutions. The first is to accept defeat and make a shady seating area or children's play area under the tree, using a bark mulch underfoot to stop weeds growing and to create a woodland atmosphere. The bark could be held in place with log edging, and you could introduce a few tubs of shade-loving plants, such as hostas, to add a little colour.

The second solution is to create a shade bed. Incorporate well-rotted organic matter into the soil to help it retain moisture and plant colourful ivies, ferns, *Epimedium* spp. (barrenwort), *Tolmiea menziesii* (pick-a-back plant), *Galanthus* spp. (snowdrops), *Saxifraga* x *urbium* (London pride) and *Pulmonaria* spp. (lungwort). Mulch the surface of the soil with more organic matter and top up every year.

▲ *Galanthus* spp. (snowdrops) will thrive in an area that is shaded for most of the year and provide a welcome patch of interest in the depths of winter.

steep banks

It is never easy to handle a lawnmower on a steep bank, and it is probably easier to try groundcover plants instead of a lawn. Be sure to choose plants that will naturally do well in the conditions on offer – check the type of soil and the amount of sun or shade the area gets. You don't have to plant a large area with just one type of plant: a mixture will create a more interesting effect as long as they are all spreading plants that will soon cover the bare soil underneath. Avoid a large number of different types, or you will end up with a bitty effect. See the groundcover plants listed on page 85.

As an alternative, consider a patch of low-mow meadow grass, especially if the bank is bordered by lawn (see pages 74–5). Allow the grass to grow long and plant a few wildflower plants and bulbs in it. You will need to strim or mow the grass once or twice a year so this solution is more labour-intensive than groundcover.

heavy clay

Although it is difficult to work, becomes waterlogged in winter and sets like concrete in summer, clay soil also has some good points. It retains moisture well in dry weather and holds nutrients, which means that it is more fertile than other, more easily worked soils. As always, the solution is to dig in as much organic matter as you can – use well-rotted farmyard manure or garden compost. Break up the lumps of clay as much as possible, preferably when the soil is just moist. This should improve the texture of the soil considerably and widen the range of plants that will grow there. However, you will still need to pick and choose, avoiding any that prefer a free-draining or drier soil. Plants that naturally prefer a heavy, moist soil include many ferns, hostas, *Hemerocallis* (daylilies), *Humulus lupulus* 'Aureus' (golden hop), *Ilex* (holly), astilbes and phlox.

▶ In any area of the garden, however much you improve the soil, it is best to choose plants that like those conditions, such as hostas and ferns for a moist site with heavy soil.

boggy ground

Naturally wet or boggy areas should be seen as a blessing, not a problem. There is a host of beautiful plants that like moist conditions, and many people create special bog gardens to accommodate them. Start by incorporating plenty of well-rotted garden compost, manure or other organic matter into the soil to improve the texture. Plant hostas, *Rheum palmatum* (Chinese rhubarb), with its huge leaves, *Zantedeschia aethiopica* (arum lily) and moisture-loving ferns in the bed. Edge it with logs or bricks, depending on the effect you want to create, and use sawn logs or irregularly shaped paving stones to create a steeping stone path through the area so that you can maintain it easily.

hot, dry corners in full sun

Many plants do better in a sunny situation than in a shady one, but few will thrive in full baking sun all day long, especially if the soil is dry. Start by improving the moisture-retention of the soil by incorporating plenty of well-rotted organic matter. Consider mulching the area with gravel, laid over thick polythene sheeting or a weed-suppressing membrane, to prevent the soil drying out. Gravel will also set off the plants well and stop weeds growing in the border. Choose Mediterranean-style, drought-resistant plants, such as rosemary, *Potentilla*, broom, *Santolina*, juniper, lavender, *Eschscholzia*, erigeron, pelargonium, pot marigold and thyme and plant through crosses cut in the membrane. See page 92 for an easy Mediterranean-style garden.

plants that look after themselves

The borders in the one-hour garden will be filled with plants that really can take care of themselves or that will thrive with the minimum attention.

No-care plants are those that will survive cold and wet winters with no ill effects; they resist the effects of drought and disease and they will perform happily without any pruning or cutting back. That's not to say they will not produce better flowers or have a better shape with a little judicious pruning, but they by no means rely on it. Easy-care plants are those that need a little bit of attention to do well, but they are well worth the minimal amount of time and effort involved. It may be they need cutting to the ground once a year, or the dead stems removed in spring before they re-emerge from their winter dormancy.

The following characteristics make plants good subjects for easy-care gardens. Before you buy anything, go through the checklist to make sure it will be suitable for your low-maintenance borders.

- Hardiness: make sure it will survive cold, wet winters.
- Slow growth: choose plants that will stay manageable without the need for constant cutting back.
- Pruning: select flowering and foliage shrubs that do not need regular pruning to perform well.
- Disease resistance: avoid plants, such as roses, that are prone to diseases.
- Staking: avoid tall, weak-stemmed perennials that cannot support themselves.
- Longevity: choose plants that will thrive for many years to come without having to be replaced.

plants to avoid

Gardeners seeking to eliminate unnecessary work will make sure that none of the following appears in their planting schemes:

- *Anchusa azurea* (alkanet): short-lived
- *Aquilegia vulgaris* (columbine, granny's bonnet): short-lived
- *Dahlia* cvs.: tender tubers need lifting for winter protection; tall cultivars need staking
- *Delphinium* cvs.: tall cultivars need staking
- *Geum* spp. (avens): needs to be divided regularly
- *Gladiolus* cvs.: tender corms need lifting for winter protection; tall cultivars need staking
- *Helenium* cvs. (sneezeweed): tall cultivars need staking
- *Rosa* cvs. (roses): need pruning to flower well; many suffer from blackspot and other diseases
- Soft fruits: need pruning and feeding to crop well

◄ *Choysia ternata* is a handsome shrub with glossy evergreen foliage and abundant white flowers. However, its most appealing feature is its wonderful fragrance.

easy ideas: an easy-care mixed border care rating ●●

▲ *Hemerocallis* flowers come in a range of striking colours, from bright red and maroon to rich orange, peach and lemon.

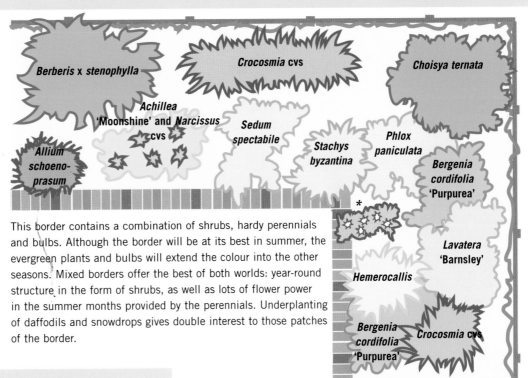

Berberis x stenophylla

Crocosmia cvs

Choisya ternata

Achillea 'Moonshine' and *Narcissus* cvs

Sedum spectabile

Stachys byzantina

Phlox paniculata

Bergenia cordifolia 'Purpurea'

Allium schoeno-prasum

*

Lavatera 'Barnsley'

Hemerocallis

Bergenia cordifolia 'Purpurea'

Crocosmia cvs

This border contains a combination of shrubs, hardy perennials and bulbs. Although the border will be at its best in summer, the evergreen plants and bulbs will extend the colour into the other seasons. Mixed borders offer the best of both worlds: year-round structure in the form of shrubs, as well as lots of flower power in the summer months provided by the perennials. Underplanting of daffodils and snowdrops gives double interest to those patches of the border.

* *Ajuga reptans* 'Burgundy Glow' and *Galanthus nivalis*

care plan

- Cut back the dead perennial foliage in early spring (or, if you want a neat garden, in autumn).

- Prune flowering shrubs every year or two to improve flowering performance.

- Water the bed if the plants wilt in dry weather.

- Apply a general fertilizer to the bed once a year in spring.

- If perennials start to look weak after several years, dig up clumps in spring, separate the vigorous bits and replant them, discarding the overgrown centre of the clump.

tips for easy-care borders

- If the border is next to a lawn, edge it with a mowing strip because the soft plants may spill out of the border at the front.

- Arrange the plants close together so there is no bare soil for weeds to colonize.

- Provide support for the clematis if the border is backed by a wall or fence. Attach trellis to the wall or fence or fix a few supporting wires to it.

easy-care plants

***Achillea* 'Moonshine'** (yarrow)

***Ajuga reptans* 'Burgundy Glow'** (bugle)

Allium schoenoprasum (chives)

Berberis x stenophylla (barberry)

***Bergenia cordifolia* 'Purpurea'** (elephant's ears)

Choisya ternata (Mexican orange blossom)

***Clematis montana* var. *rubens* 'Tetrarose'**

***Crocosmia* cvs.** (montbretia)

Galanthus nivalis (snowdrop)

Hemerocallis (daylily)

***Lavatera* 'Barnsley'** (mallow)

***Narcissus* cvs.** (daffodil)

Phlox paniculata

Sedum spectabile (ice plant)

Stachys byzantina (lamb's ears)

fuss-free foliage

Foliage acts as a foil to flowering plants, creating balance in a border, but many foliage plants can be attractive in their own right, bringing colour and grace to your planting scheme. Use a variety of different colours and leaf shapes among flowers in a border or create an all-foliage tapestry of varying greens that will be restful and beautiful.

A garden without flowers, or with only a few flowers, need never be dull. Foliage plants can provide all the interest you could possibly want. It would be a mistake to think of foliage plants as being all green. Not only is there a tremendous range of greens, from the bright apple green of *Epimedium* (barrenwort) to the blue-green of *Alchemilla mollis* (lady's mantle) and the dark, glossy green of *Fatsia japonica* (Japanese aralia), there is the brilliant silver, yellow and gold variegation seen in aucubas and euonymus. There are also every possible texture, shape and habit of growth, from rounded hummocks of moss to fountains of spiky cordylines and grasses.

Ornamental grasses are much in vogue, and they are a remarkably resilient and tolerant group of plants, which require nothing more than a once-a-year haircut. A mixed grass border can be an effective and low-maintenance feature, as well as being attractive. Vary the heights, colours and shapes of the grasses for best effect. Many die back in the winter, but the brown stems are attractive and retain structure until you cut them off in spring. Grasses create a pleasant rustling sound in breezy weather, and produce handsome seedheads in summer and autumn.

Foliage plants in general need less attention than flowering ones – there is no need to deadhead for a start – and trees and shrubs need far less maintenance than herbaceous perennials and hardy annuals. Provided the ground is thoroughly prepared at planting time and the plants are surrounded by a good mulch, they will repay the effort with years of handsome leaves for no further work.

easy ideas: a fuss-free foliage scheme care rating ●●

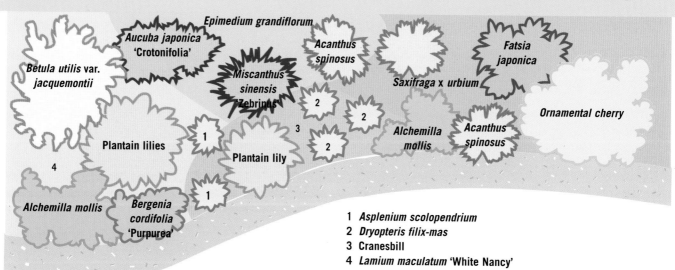

1 *Asplenium scolopendrium*
2 *Dryopteris filix-mas*
3 *Cranesbill*
4 *Lamium maculatum* 'White Nancy'

The fuss-free foliage scheme is much like a mixed border (see page 89), but it makes use of a wide range of handsome foliage plants in order to create a restful display. The trees in the border create shade for the smaller plants beneath, but if your border is already shady, you won't need to add any more, so replace the trees detailed here with some of the easy-care shrubs that are listed on pages 142–3.

A few evergreen shrubs and perennials add winter interest, as do the ornamental barks of the trees selected for this scheme. Some of the plants are used in large drifts to act as a sort of groundcover, but the drifts are sometimes punctuated by stately ferns, which pop up through them to add a bit of height. Although the border design concentrates on foliage, many of the plants also produce flowers to add to the interest.

▲ *Lamium maculatum* 'White Nancy' creates a silver cushion of foliage throughout the year. White flowers appear in the summer.
▶ Hostas come in a wide range of colours and bicolours and are here nicely offset by contrasting spiky foliage.

fuss-free foliage plants

Acanthus spinosus (bear's breeches)
Alchemilla mollis (lady's mantle)
Asplenium scolopendrium (hart's tongue fern)
Aucuba japonica 'Crotonifolia' (spotted laurel)
Bergenia cordifolia 'Purpurea' (elephant's ears)
Betula utilis var. jacquemontii (Himalayan birch)
Dryopteris filix-mas (male fern)
Epimedium grandiflorum (barrenwort)
Fatsia japonica (Japanese aralia)
Geranium macrorrhizum
Hosta sieboldiana var. elegans
Lamium maculatum 'White Nancy' (deadnettle)
Miscanthus sinensis 'Zebrinus' (zebra grass)
Saxifraga x urbium (London pride)

time-saving tips

● Prepare the soil well before planting, adding plenty of organic matter to get the plants off to a good start.

● Arrange the plants close together to avoid any patches of bare soil.

● Mulch the soil to retain moisture and suppress weeds.

care plan

● Cut back the dead perennial foliage in early spring.

● Top up the mulch each spring.

● Apply a general fertilizer every year or two.

easy ideas: a mediterranean planting care rating ●●

▲ A Mediterranean planting scheme will include robust-looking plants that need very little attention throughout the year.

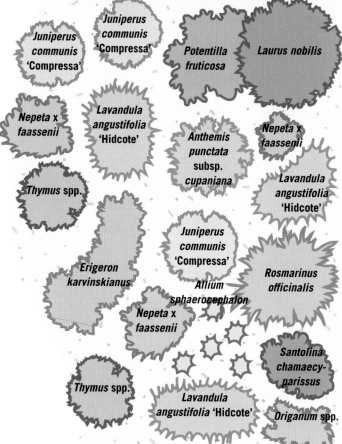

Juniperus communis 'Compressa'

Juniperus communis 'Compressa'

Potentilla fruticosa

Laurus nobilis

Nepeta x faassenii

Lavandula angustifolia 'Hidcote'

Anthemis punctata subsp. cupaniana

Nepeta x faassenii

Thymus spp.

Lavandula angustifolia 'Hidcote'

Juniperus communis 'Compressa'

Erigeron karvinskianus

Allium sphaerocephalon

Rosmarinus officinalis

Nepeta x faassenii

Santolina chamaecyparissus

Thymus spp.

Lavandula angustifolia 'Hidcote'

Origanum spp.

plants for a mediterranean garden

Allium sphaerocephalon (ornamental onion)

Anthemis punctata subsp. **cupaniana**

Erigeron karvinskianus (fleabane)

Juniperus communis 'Compressa' (common juniper)

Laurus nobilis (bay)

Lavandula angustifolia 'Hidcote' (lavender)

Nepeta x faassenii (catmint)

Origanum spp. (oregano)

Potentilla fruticosa (cinquefoil)

Rosmarinus officinalis (rosemary)

Santolina chamaecyparissus (cotton lavender)

Thymus spp. (thyme)

Plants that are native to countries around the Mediterranean are naturally drought-resistant and tough, making them good choices for the one-hour garden. Many have silvery foliage, which is offset beautifully by gravel, so a gravel mulch will add to the effect. All of these plants will revel in a hot, sunny corner, tolerating dry conditions and full sun. See pages 74–5 for advice on planting a gravel garden.

care plan

● Shear over the lavender, *Santolina* (cotton lavender) and anthemis in early spring to improve flowering performance.

● Remove dead foliage from *Nepeta* (catmint), erigeron and oregano in autumn or early spring.

● Top up the gravel mulch as necessary.

time-saving tips

● Lay polythene sheeting or a weed-suppressing membrane over the areas to be gravelled.

● Prepare the soil well before planting, adding plenty of organic matter to increase its moisture retention and help the plants tolerate drought even better.

● Leave spaces between the plants to create a more relaxed effect – the gravel will prevent weeds appearing.

easy ideas: a year-round shrub border care rating ●●

Shrubs are among the most useful plants for the one-hour garden. They suppress weeds, are fairly drought-resistant and, once they are established, do not require constant feeding, staking or deadheading. A shrub border is an easy form of permanent planting that involves little effort but that provides plenty of structure and year-round interest.

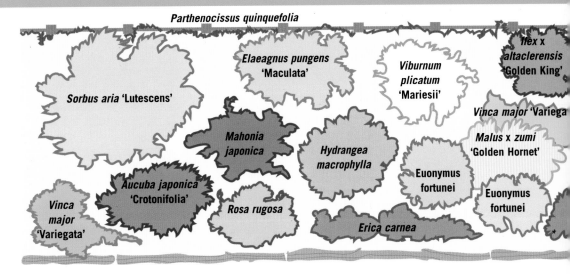

Parthenocissus quinquefolia

Sorbus aria 'Lutescens'

Elaeagnus pungens 'Maculata'

Viburnum plicatum 'Mariesii'

Ilex x altaclerensis 'Golden King'

Vinca major 'Variega

Malus x zumi 'Golden Hornet'

Mahonia japonica

Hydrangea macrophylla

Euonymus fortunei

Euonymus fortunei

Aucuba japonica 'Crotonifolia'

Rosa rugosa

Vinca major 'Variegata'

Erica carnea

* Erica carnea

plants for the year-round shrub border

Aucuba japonica 'Crotonifolia' (spotted laurel)

Elaeagnus pungens 'Maculata'

Erica carnea (heather)

Euonymus fortunei 'Emerald 'n' Gold' (spindle)

Hydrangea macrophylla

Ilex x altaclerensis 'Golden King' (holly)

Mahonia japonica

Malus x zumi 'Golden Hornet' (crabapple)

Parthenocissus quinquefolia (Virginia creeper)

Rosa rugosa (hedgehog rose)

Sorbus aria 'Lutescens' (whitebeam)

Viburnum plicatum 'Mariesii' (Japanese snowball bush)

Vinca major 'Variegata' (periwinkle)

care plan

- Prune flowering shrubs every year or two to improve flowering performance.
- Sweep up fallen leaves from deciduous shrubs in autumn.
- Apply a general fertilizer to the bed once a year in spring.
- Top up the mulch as necessary.

time-saving tips

- Mulch the border to cover the soil and prevent weed growth while the shrubs are filling out.
- Don't plant the shrubs too close together or you will be cutting them back after a few years.
- Choose tough, hardy shrubs because if they don't survive they will be expensive to replace.
- Choose plants with a compact habit so you won't need to cut them back to keep them in shape.
- Choose plants that don't rely on yearly pruning to stay looking good.
- Prepare the soil well before planting to get the shrubs off to a good start.

▲ Hydrangeas are large, handsome rounded shrubs that produce a colourful display of summer flowers.

fail-safe containers

Containers are a boon to the one-hour gardener because they make it possible to grow a wide range of plants without the work involved in planting and maintaining a full-scale border. They are generally quite low on labour, but they are invaluable for bringing life and colour to what might otherwise be dull stretches of paving or decking. The main drawback is their need for regular watering, but even this need not be a constant chore with a little forethought and care (see pages 96–7 for some shortcuts).

Plants in containers are easily reached for tending, and you can grow just about anything you like in a container, even when your garden soil is unsuitable – gardeners who have alkaline soil, for example, can grow azaleas or camellias in containers and enjoy their lovely spring blooms. Containers also offer better protection against slugs, snails and other soil-borne pests.

As the plants come in and out of flower you can move containers around, so the displays in your border are always colourful and full of interest. You can even empty them if you get tired of the plants and use the containers themselves as decorative elements in your garden.

▲ Large containers, especially those made of impermeable material, retain moisture much better than small terracotta pots. The trick when using containers in an easy-care garden is to group them so that you spend as little time as possible walking to and fro with a watering can.
◄ Containers need not just be used for bedding plants: these ornamental grasses make a simple yet striking arrangement.
► These ranked tiers of large metal containers make a striking background to the tiled water feature, keeping a sense of order even with plants that can look unruly, such as nasturtiums and tomatoes.

golden rules for easy containers

- Choose containers carefully. Large containers need less frequent watering than small ones and some materials, such as terracotta, dry out much more quickly than others. Avoid wide, shallow containers, lots of small pots and, especially, hanging baskets, all of which need frequent watering.

- Choose the right type of compost. The compost needs to be free-draining to avoid waterlogging but still retain moisture around the plants' roots. Multi-purpose compost is too lightweight for use for most plants, especially for permanent displays, and is difficult to re-wet once it has dried out. Mix it, half and half, with a soil-based compost for bedding displays or use a suitable soil-based compost alone for shrubs and permanent plantings. Try to buy peat-free composts where possible.

- Group containers together to make tending them easier, rather than having them dotted about the garden. This will also result in a display with more impact and cut down on the amount of moisture lost from their compost, so it should save you time on watering.

- Choose easy-care plants that will tolerate a little neglect now and again and be happy with slightly dry conditions.

- Include some permanent elements in your containers so you don't have to start from scratch and replace all the plants every season. Evergreens are most suitable.

choosing containers

material	pros	cons	tips
cement and reconstituted stone	Some are very attractive Retains moisture better than terracotta	Some styles are hideous Heavy Can be expensive	Plant up *in situ* so that you do not have to move them when full of compost
ceramic	Available in a range of attractive styles and colours More free-draining than plastic but more water-retentive than terracotta	Fairly expensive Not always frostproof	Buy the largest size you can afford
fibreglass	Reproductions of antique lead containers and urns are attractive	Expensive	Use a single specimen plant so as not to detract from the container
plastic	Inexpensive Retains moisture well	Unattractive Easy to overwater	Avoid for plants that like dry conditions because it is easy to overwater
terracotta	Attractive Comparatively light Difficult to overwater Suits most plant types and garden styles	Loses moisture quickly Not always frostproof Can be expensive	Use for plants that are drought tolerant or line the inside with polythene or waterproof paint

feeding shortcuts

Container-grown plants, whether they are temporary bedding or permanent shrubs and perennials, rely on you for food and water. The nutrients that are added to bags of compost last for about eight weeks, so after that it's up to you. For bedding displays that require lots of feed for maximum flowering you will have to apply a liquid feed every three or four weeks. It is easier to buy slow-release feed pellets or spikes, which can be inserted into the compost and which will slowly release the necessary nutrients over a period of several months.

Feeding is also important for shrubs and perennials in containers, although they won't shrivel up and die if you are sometimes forgetful. Aim to apply a handful of a good general-purpose fertilizer, such as pelleted chicken manure, once a year in spring. Fork it into the top of the compost.

watering shortcuts

- Choose large containers to reduce evaporation.

- Leave at least 2.5cm (1in) at the top of the pot to fill up when watering.

- Water thoroughly each time you do it.

- Mulch the top of the pot with gravel or cobbles to retain moisture in the compost.

- In very hot weather put each pot in a saucer but make sure that it is not constantly standing in water, and remove the saucer in autumn so that the compost does not get waterlogged.

- Use self-watering containers, which have a water reservoir and capillary matting at the bottom to keep the compost moist for up to two weeks.

- Group containers together to retain a moist atmosphere around them.

- Add moisture-retaining granules to the compost when you are planting. These lock in moisture and let it out slowly when the compost becomes dry.

- Install an automatic watering system if you have lots of containers. These systems consist of a series of fine tubes running from the tubs to a tap. They can be turned on and off as necessary or operated by a simple timer.

- Make sure there are drainage holes in the container so that excess water can drain away. Waterlogged compost will kill many plants and will freeze in winter, killing the plants and cracking the container.

- Raise containers off the ground to allow water to drain away freely.

top-dressing

It is a good idea to replace the top 2.5–5cm (1–2in) of compost in a container of permanent planting each year. Do this in spring, carefully removing the top section of soil, so that you do not damage the roots, and replacing it with new compost. Water thoroughly and top up with a layer of gravel.

permanent plantings

Almost any plant can be grown in a container, and you certainly don't have to stick to traditional bedding species, such as petunias and lobelias. These displays require a lot of work – intensive watering and feeding, plus a complete replanting at least once, sometimes twice, a year if they are to look their best all year round. If you particularly like these flower-filled container displays, follow the watering and feeding outlined opposite – but you will have to be prepared for some extra work.

Small trees, shrubs, flowers and foliage plants are a better choice for the busy gardener. Aim to choose plants that will be happy with relatively dry soil so that you don't have to water them every day in warm weather. Some plants have adapted to survive with relatively little moisture – those from Mediterranean regions, for example – and these are great choices for containers (see page 92 for some ideas). Make sure that you choose plants that will survive winter wet and cold as well.

Permanent plantings can be quite colourful, but they do create a different effect from busy bedding schemes. They tend to have a more mature look and often rely as much on foliage as flowers to maintain year-round appeal. Unless the container is large, it is usual to have just one type of plant in each, but the containers can be grouped to create a mini-border. Choose a selection of plants that will have something to offer in every season, even if it is just handsome foliage or a framework of stark woody stems.

◀ Permanent container displays need feeding once a year. This one contains a variegated holly and *Alchemilla mollis*.
▶ *Buxus sempervirens* (box) bushes in pots can add structure to the garden all year. If you choose a slow-growing variety, it will only need clipping once a year.

year-round displays

Year-round displays mix permanent planting with bedding and offer a good compromise for many. They contain a few permanent elements to keep containers looking good throughout the year and to minimize the replanting, but a few bedding plants are added to these for seasonal colour and extra flowers. Bulbs are a good choice to add a splash of colour or choose easy-care pansies or pelargoniums for a longer period of flowers. Combine these with evergreens, such as juniper, *Hedera* (ivy), *Aucuba japonica* (spotted laurel), *Berberis* (barberry) or *Bergenia* (elephant's ears), for the permanent elements.

container recipes instant edibles

▲ A glazed terracotta strawberry pot makes a decorative feature out of an aubergine plant and a few herbs.

ingredients

bucket to mix compost in
multipurpose compost
soil-based compost
glazed terracotta strawberry pot
a few small stones or pieces of broken flowerpot
5 small French parsley plants
1 aubergine plant
slow-release feed pellets
3 canes, plus a cane top

This handsome tub contains aubergines and French parsley to keep you in fresh produce all summer long. Buying small plants from a garden centre rather than trying to grow them from seed makes this an instant display, which is quick and easy to plant. The glazed pot will retain moisture better than plain terracotta, so you won't have to water it so often. Use a mixture of multipurpose and soil-based compost to combine the best qualities of each; multipurpose compost dries out quickly and is difficult to re-wet once dry. Use slow-release feed pellets so you won't have to bother with a weekly feed.

how to plant

1 Mix equal quantities of multipurpose and soil-based compost in a bucket.

2 Place small stones or pieces of broken flowerpot over the drainage holes in the bottom of the pot, then half-fill the pot with the compost mixture, firming it down lightly.

3 Remove the parsley plants from their pots one at a time and tease most of the compost away from around their roots, so the rootballs are small enough to slip into the holes in the sides of the pot.

4 Firm the compost around their roots and top up the container with more compost, almost to the rim.

5 Plant the aubergine plant in the top of the pot and insert the feed pellets, following the directions on the packet. Add more compost, firming it lightly until the top of the compost is about 2.5cm (1in) below the rim of the container.

6 Insert the three canes into the compost around the pot rim and bring the tops together in the centre of the pot. Secure them in place with the cane top. Water well.

spring display

This display combines deliciously scented narcissi and creamy yellow pansies. It will bring welcome colour into the garden in early spring before much else is around. The narcissi and trails of variegated ivy are permanent features – the ivy adds colour and interest all year, while the narcissi come up every spring to give a wonderful show. The pansies add seasonal colour and can be replaced with more pansies or other bedding plants as they fade.

ingredients

container
small stone
soil-based compost
12 *Narcissus* 'Bridal Crown' bulbs
6 *Viola* 'Universal Primrose' plants
3 variegated ivy plants, such as *Hedera helix* 'Goldchild'
slow-release feed pellets

how to plant

1 Place a small stone over the drainage hole in the bottom of the container to prevent the compost leaching out. Fill the container with compost up to about 12.5cm (5in) below the rim of the pot and firm lightly.

2 Space the bulbs evenly over the surface of the compost with the tips uppermost. Cover with compost to within 5cm (2in) of the pot rim.

3 Plant the pansies in the top of the pot, five evenly spaced around the edges and one in the middle.

4 Space the ivies roughly around the edges of the pot and fill in the gaps between the rootballs with more compost.

5 Firm the compost lightly between the plants and top it up so the surface is 2.5cm (1in) below the rim of the pot. Insert the slow-release feed pellets according to the instructions on the packet and water the tub well.

evergreen tub

This is the ultimate easy-care container display that looks good all year round and won't need replanting for years to come. Although the plants are evergreen, the display really changes with the seasons, adding interest at different times of year. The skimmia at the back is a small shrub with glossy foliage all year round. In autumn and winter it produces rich red buds that open into frothy white flowers in spring. Choose a female variety, which will also bear bright red berries after the flowers have faded. Euphorbia is another evergreen – this one has handsome reddish foliage and has large heads of acid yellow flowers in late spring. The flowers contrast sharply with the purplish foliage, creating a dramatic effect, and last for many months.

ingredients

tall container
small stone or piece of broken flowerpot
soil-based compost
1 *Skimmia japonica* plant
1 *Euphorbia amygdaloides* 'Purpurea' plant
2 variegated ivy plants, such as *Hedera helix* 'Goldchild'

how to plant

1 Place a small stone or piece of broken flowerpot over the drainage hole in the bottom of the container. Fill the container with compost to about three-quarters full, then firm lightly.

2 Remove the skimmia from its pot and plant at the back of the container. Plant the euphorbia in front of it.

3 Add more compost around the rootballs of the plants, firming gently. The tops of both of the rootballs should be about 2.5cm (1in) below the rim of the container.

4 Plant the ivy plants in the top of the container, one either side of the euphorbia. Fill the gaps between the plants with more compost and firm gently. Water well.

easy edibles

There are few things more satisfying than popping out into the garden to pick a handful of fresh vegetables or succulent fruit for lunch. However, most vegetables and fruits require attention if they are going to produce a decent crop, so easy-care gardeners are rather limited in their choice. If you want to grow a few crisp lettuces, sweet baby carrots or crunchy fine beans you are in luck, however, and most herbs also fall into the easy-care category. The only fruits that really look after themselves are alpine strawberries and rhubarb, both of which come up year after year without any help at all.

◄ Planted in rows in a raised bed vegetables can also make an attractive border in a garden.

where to grow

Most herbs, vegetables and salad plants require a sunny site and free-draining soil, and raised beds are ideal, because the soil won't be trodden on, making digging unnecessary, and the plants are easily reached. This is a good choice if your garden soil is unsuitable as you can fill the bed with appropriate fresh soil and compost.

You can also dot vegetables, herbs and fruits about among other plants in the border – many are decorative – or you can create small beds specially for edibles, but follow the golden rules on page 103.

Many herbs and vegetables can be grown in containers; see pages 102–3 for more details. Growbags are a simple solution, although they are not especially attractive. They come ready filled with nutrient-rich compost and the plants are planted through holes cut in the top. Stand a few pots in front of them to hide the plastic bag.

what to grow: easy herbs

- Bay is a well-known herb. Established plants have masses of leaves and make attractive garden shrubs.

- Chives are easy-to-grow herbs that come up every year with plenty of onion-flavoured foliage. Grow this decorative plant in any border.

- Fennel is another attractive perennial herb, which produces tall, wispy fronds and yellow flowers every year. Grow it among flowers to provide height in the border. Remove seedheads to prevent self-sowing and cut back dead stems in early spring.

- Mint is a reliable, pretty perennial plant but one that spreads rapidly if the roots are not contained. There are many different flavours and leaf colours available.

- Oregano or common marjoram is another leafy herb that comes up year after year. It has mid-green or lime-green foliage and lilac flowers. Remove seed-heads to prevent self-sowing and remove any dead stems in spring.

- Rosemary is an evergreen herb that makes an attractive garden plant with blue or pink flowers in spring. Pick off the leaves as you need them.

- Thyme, another evergreen herb, forms cushions of foliage with pink or mauve flowers in summer. Pick sprigs as required.

what to grow: easy fruit, vegetables and salads

- Alpine strawberries produce small, sweet fruits through summer and autumn. Plants are decorative but invasive; pull out any that appear in the wrong place.

- Broad beans will grow from large seeds, which are popped in the ground in early spring. The succulent beans can be picked several weeks later. Pick just before eating for maximum sweetness.

- Carrots grow from fine seed, sown in late spring. The roots swell into sweet, crisp carrots. Use when tiny in salads or allow to grow larger.

- French beans are also known as snap, string and kidney beans. Sow the big seeds in spring and pick the juicy pods later in the season. Make sure you select bush cultivars unless you are growing them up trellis or canes, and choose stringless types.

- Lettuces will be ready from as little as seven weeks after sowing. Sow a few seeds at a time from late spring onwards and watch the lettuces form. Choose pick-and-come-again cultivars so you can harvest only as many leaves as you need.

- Onions can be grown from either seed or sets; both should be planted in late winter to early spring according to type for a supply from midsummer on.

- Radishes are one of the fastest edibles to grow. Simply sow a little seed every few weeks from late spring onwards and pull up the crisp, sweet radishes as they swell.

- Rhubarb is a handsome plant that comes up every year. Harvest the pink stems in late spring.

- Rocket can be sown in the same way as lettuces, from late spring onwards. Pick off the peppery leaves as you need them when the plants reach a reasonable size.

◄ Once they are established, onions require relatively little care, although they will need watering regularly for a few weeks after planting out.

edibles in containers

Containers provide a simple alternative way of growing quick and easy edibles, including herbs, vegetables and fruits, without the back-breaking work of a vegetable patch.

The easy-care gardener will avoid the vegetable patch: above all garden features, the traditional vegetable plot, consisting of row after row of vegetables with bare soil between them, is the one-hour gardener's worst nightmare. Such plots need to be dug over regularly to loosen the soil before the next crop is put in, and well-rotted compost or manure has to be dug in every year. In intensively cultivated vegetable plots crops have to be rotated so that pests and diseases are avoided and the ground does not become depleted of nutrients. Then the bare soil between the plants must be weeded, which will involve walking on the soil to get between the rows, which compacts it and creates the need for more digging. But perhaps more importantly: who's got time to care for lots of vegetables and fruit?

Instead, keep your herbs and vegetables in pots. Containers are much more flexible: you can use as many or few as you like so that you can vary your growing space with the changing seasons, without leaving bare soil to worry about. Plants are more accessible in containers and you won't need to dig the soil – simply renew it or fork it over and replenish the nutrients between each planting. If the compost is rich enough, plant the plants close together to suppress weeds in the tubs and increase your yield. Slugs and snails are easier to control in containers than in the open garden, so you may get some perfect lettuce leaves.

The easiest and most productive edibles for containers are alpine strawberries, bay, chives, French beans, lettuces, rocket, thyme and tomatoes.

save time

- Arrange the plants close together in the containers to suppress weeds and retain moisture.

- Keep the plants well watered and fed to avoid pests and diseases, which will take time to deal with.

- Consider installing an automatic watering system if you have a lot of containers.

- Use long-lasting feed pellets specially designed for containers, which will last for some time before they need to be renewed or supplemented.

- Water the containers thoroughly each time you do it to reduce the overall watering needed.

- Stand several containers in a group – edibles or not – to retain moisture around them.

- When planting, mix water-retaining crystals into the compost to help retain moisture.

◄ Herbs are attractive plants in their own right. Here they are displayed to good effect in a group of painted pots, close to the kitchen door for easy picking.

◄ The contrasting leaves of chives, marjoram, thyme and sage make a pretty group within the strong lines of a galvanized metal container.

golden rules for easy edibles

- Choose easy-care vegetables, herbs and fruits that don't require any special attention, apart from the initial sowing or planting.

- Avoid traditional vegetable patches with rows of plants separated by earth paths. By treading on the soil, you make regular digging necessary, and the bare soil is weed heaven.

- Be selective. Grow just a few choice edibles as they are notoriously time-consuming.

- Plant close together to smother weeds; grow in blocks rather than rows for best effect.

- Keep vegetable beds small so you can reach all the plants from a path or other firm surface.

- Sow small quantities at a time to avoid gluts. Seed of salad crops, such as lettuces and radishes, can be sown every three or four weeks so you have just a few maturing at a time.

- Keep the soil fertile for high yields.

enjoy it

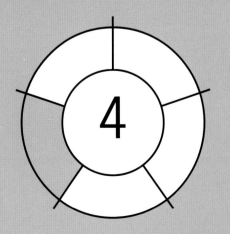

For many people the most important function of a garden is as an extra room where it is possible for the whole family to relax, play, lounge around, eat alfresco and entertain friends and family, and you should now have plenty of time on your hands for rest and relaxation in your own garden.

An outdoor room is exactly what the name suggests: an extension of the house that can be used for whatever purpose best reflects your lifestyle. The only difference between an indoor and an outdoor room is that outside you have to accommodate the weather, and this means providing surfaces for all-weather use and protection from the wind and rain. A lawn is often too wet to sit on, so you need a large area of an all-weather surface, such as paving, decking or gravel, that can be used for dining, lounging about, playing and even preparing and cooking food. If you spend a lot of time outside, you will want as large an area of hard surface as possible (which will also cut down on the work you will have to do in the garden), in a sheltered, preferably sunny site, with some shade for hot weather. You might also want a shaded, private place in the garden, where you can sit peacefully, reading or dozing, shielded from the activities of the rest of the family.

Alfresco eating is becoming increasingly popular. This may require nothing more than a simple, flat area where you can stand a table and chairs safely so that people can enjoy food that has been cooked indoors, but it is more often likely to involve a barbecue, either a free-standing model or a small, purpose-built one. The provision of garden furniture is big business these days, which means that there is a wide choice of styles, materials and prices to suit every type of garden layout – including the one-hour garden, which needs accessories that are easy to look after and easy to use.

'an outdoor room is exactly what the name suggests: an extension of the house that can be used for whatever purpose best reflects your lifestyle'

◄ Although terracotta containers should generally be avoided, you can cut down on the amount of time it takes to water them by grouping them or by lining the inside of the pots with plastic.

▲ Garden furniture should be as decorative as it is functional. It can be used to help create the garden style you want to achieve.
◀ The dense planting in this outdoor room, although including exotic specimens, gives it a cosy, intimate atmosphere.

keeping the children happy

If you have a young family it is important to plan the garden with the children in mind from the beginning, because they are likely to use it more than you are. A garden should offer a safe place for them to play, climb trees, kick a ball about or ride a bicycle, while under your supervision.

The key to successful planning for children is to provide what they would like and not what you would like. If they are old enough, ask them what they want and get them involved in the planning process. Children are often happy with the simplest of things, such as an open space to play on and a secret place in some dense bushes, which they can adapt for all kinds of real and imaginary games. Structures such as climbing frames and sandpits should be designed with the child in mind, rather than being selected because they will fit into the garden design or look attractive. With a little

forethought, however, you might be able to provide something that can be turned into another feature once the children have outgrown it. A wooden climbing frame, for example, could be clad with timber and transformed into a shed or summerhouse, while a playhouse might have a second useful life as a bicycle shed or store. If you are careful, you will site such items with this later, alternative use in mind.

In a small garden you will probably have to make provision for the children in the general garden, and this usually means having a the lawn or area covered with a thick layer of bark chippings for their climbing frame, swings and toys. In a larger garden you may be able to set aside an area especially for them, perhaps with a sandpit, paddling pool, swing, slide and even a treehouse.

sandpits

Sandpits never seem to go out of favour with children, who will spend hours building castles and knocking them down again. Special sand is available for play; it will not stain clothes and does not contain sharp flints. With care, it is possible to build a sandpit in such a way that it can be turned into a garden pond once it is no longer wanted as a sandpit. Both, for different reasons, need to be sited in a sunny position within clear view of the house.

keeping them in

One of the most important aspects of safety in the garden is making sure that the children stay there. A child wandering unnoticed on to a road or away from house is susceptible to all kinds of problems and potential accidents. Make sure that the garden is surrounded by an adequate boundary of some sort and that all gates are firmly shut and locked with child-proof or out-of-reach catches. Make sure that a child cannot slip through the bars of a gate or fence, and check that visitors, such as the postman, cannot accidentally leave the gate open.

◄ Sandpits provide hours of fun and entertainment. This one is surrounded by paving so the stray sand can simply be swept back in after play.

getting them interested

As well as providing children with somewhere they can play safely, a well-designed and well-used garden will instil a love of gardening. One way to encourage children to be interested is to help them to create their own garden. Lack of interest in boring repetitive jobs and short attention spans make children good one-hour gardeners, but they need the incentive of instant plants rather than the prospect of long-term spare time. Encourage them with quick-growing annual plants and vegetables, so that they have the interest of something always changing.

garden safety for children

- Make sure that all gates can be securely latched and that all boundaries are intact.

- Create a soft landing under play equipment by laying a material such as chipped bark to a depth of 5–8cm (2–3in).

- Site young children's play equipment where it can be seen from the house.

- Avoid poisonous, prickly and stinging plants. Many garden centres now label poisonous plants, but be sure to ask if you are at all uncertain.

- Features with open water should be fenced off or covered with a strong grid. Alternatively, install a bubble fountain.

- Protect children from injury from greenhouse or other glass, sharp canes and sticks.

▲ *Digitalis purpurea* (foxgloves) are poisonous, so avoid growing them in a garden where children may play.

poisonous plants

Aconitum spp. (aconite, monkshood)
Arum spp. (lords and ladies)
Brugmansia syn. Datura (angel's trumpets)
Colchicum spp. (autumn crocus)
Digitalis spp. (foxglove)
Euphorbia spp. (spurge)
Laburnum spp.
Rhamnus spp. (buckthorn)
Solanum spp.
Taxus spp. (yew)

creating shade

In hot, sunny weather it can be uncomfortable to sit in the sun for prolonged periods, especially if you are having a meal outside or simply relaxing with a book. The dappled shade of a pergola or shady bower is much more pleasant and creates a more convivial atmosphere for entertaining. If your garden already has patches of shade, site your sitting areas in them; if not, there are many ways you can create a shady spot.

◀ An awning or blind fixed to the wall and held on thin canes provides the simplest form of shade for a little corner.

permanent shade

structure	pros	cons	tips
arbour	Round or square so perfect for a small dining area; can have a solid roof or slats and available in many materials	Open structure means that there is little shelter from wind	More open designs need climbers to create shade
pergola	Ideal for shading a seating area and creating intimate atmosphere; can be built to fit any space and different materials are available	Uprights should be concreted into the ground	Cover with climbing plants to create dappled shade
summerhouse	Pleasant place to dine in comfort, wide range of styles and sizes available	Expensive	Place some way from the house if possible for privacy
trees	Create cool, dappled shade, deciduous trees give the best shade	Sizes vary and some trees will shade a whole garden, evergreens cast deep shade	Raise the crown of large trees to minimize the shade

temporary shade

Temporary shade, in the form of awnings, parasols and canvas gazebos, is flexible and is a great idea if you only have space for one seating area because you can use it when you like. These temporary structures also make perfect sense for parties when you want a larger area of shade than normal, perhaps in the middle of the lawn where there is more space. Awnings, parasols and gazebos can be packed away when not in use.

Canvas gazebos, which are rather like tents stretched over a simple metal frame, are becoming increasingly popular. They have a top supported on four narrow legs, and optional side panels are available. These structures are also quite effective for keeping out bad weather, making them useful for parties.

An awning is usually attached to a wall on one side with a couple of long poles on the other to hold up the front. It can be pulled down and supported on the poles when needed and rolled up when not in use. Awnings are ideal for patios adjoining the house. Usually made of canvas or split bamboo, awnings can be home-made from brightly coloured sheets, canvas or split bamboo blinds. Use long canes or poles and string to support them, but remember to attach simple guy ropes to avoid disaster in breezy weather.

Parasols – giant canvas umbrellas – are easy to put up and down and can be moved around the garden at will. They need a heavy base to hold them upright and do not usually create a very large area of shade, but their flexibility makes them useful nonetheless.

choosing a simple pergola

- Rustic pergolas are easy to erect as the poles can be cut to size and nailed together. Use preservative-treated poles, and if you wish colour them with woodstain.

- Sawn timber pergolas are readily available in kit form, with the uprights and rails already cut to size and shape. Designs vary, and you can personalize them with coloured woodstain.

- Tubular metal pergolas can be painted or coated with plastic to make them more durable. Some are rather thin and lightweight and will rust much more quickly than good-quality models.

- Wrought iron creates a strong, heavy feature that will last many years. It must also be painted or coated to prevent rust.

- Brick piers supporting overhead wooden poles make a large, handsome pergola with a Mediterranean flavour. Use pressure-treated wood.

top 10 plants for creating shade

Betula utilis var. *jacquemontii* (Himalayan birch)
Clematis montana var. *rubens* 'Tetrarose'
Humulus lupulus 'Aureus' (golden hop)
Lonicera periclymenum (honeysuckle)
Malus domestica (apple)
Malus x *zumi* 'Golden Hornet' (crabapple)
Prunus serrula (ornamental cherry/birch bark tree)
Sorbus aria 'Lutescens' (whitebeam)
Viburnum plicatum 'Mariesii' (Japanese snowball bush)
Vitis spp. (vine)

◄ This honeysuckle (*Lonicera periclymenum* 'Serotina') creates good shade, and has the added bonus of scented flowers. Plant around a seating area where it can really be appreciated.

entertaining

Even better than relaxing and enjoying the warm weather in your own garden is sharing the experience with your friends and family. Whether the occasion is a drinks party, afternoon tea, a long lazy lunch or a full-blown candlelit dinner under the stars, the outdoor room will come into its own, and you know that your garden will be looking its best.

◄ This deck is large enough to accommodate a table and chairs in spacious comfort. Create as much sitting space as you can – you will use more than you think.

eating out

Many people feel more comfortable eating in an enclosed space than in the open. Although they may not actually want to be indoors, they prefer an enclosed space of some sort. This could be provided by shrubs and trees in a little glade or by an arbour. On the other hand, the skeleton outline of a room, provided by the four posts and crossbars of a pergola, my be sufficient to create the illusion of space. Such a framework is even better if it is clad with a climber to provide some pleasant shade. Fragrant plants are essential, whether they are climbers, such as honeysuckle or jasmine, or tubs of lilies or tobacco plants nearby. In the evening the structure can be used to support lights. Even sitting on a small terrace rather than on a bare expanse of lawn somehow seems to define space and make people feel more comfortable. Make an effort to dress the table for special occasions – crisp napkins and fresh flowers make the great outdoors seem more civilized.

practical pointers

- Have a permanent dining table and chairs if you have the space; just add a tablecloth and seat cushions when you want to eat.

- Position the table on a firm, flat surface so that it stands steady.

- Fold-away tables are useful in small spaces.

- Get as large a table as possible so there is plenty of room for plates of food and for everyone to sit in comfort.

- Choose comfortable chairs, with added cushions for long alfresco meals. Make sure they are at the right height for the table.

- If you eat outside quite often, site the dining area close to the kitchen so that you don't have to walk the full length of the garden with every plate of food.

- Provide either permanent or temporary shade for dining – hot sunshine is very uncomfortable (see pages 110–11).

cooking in the open air

Depending on the type and scale of the entertaining you do in your garden, you might want to plan to have a barbecue on the patio. This could be a permanent, built-in feature, perhaps with integral seating and storage, or a mobile one, which will have to be stored in the shed or garage when it is not needed. In many ways, a mobile barbecue is more convenient because you will have the flexibility to move it to the most suitable position for the occasion. It is the working centre of the party, and the cook will want to be as close as possible to the guests.

A built-in barbecue can be as simple or as sophisticated as you wish, ranging from a simple brick hearth to a more complex structure that includes a flue, and somewhere to store equipment and tools.

barbecue hints and tips

- Barbecuing is a fun, easy way to entertain, but is also great for family meals.

- Barbecues can be free-standing or built-in and as simple or complicated as you like. Decide which features you will use before you buy one.

- Free-standing barbecues can be moved around to accommodate the weather, but need to be stored away in winter, so before you buy make sure you have somewhere to keep your mobile barbecue.

- Built-in barbecues can have accompanying work surfaces, cupboards for storing tools and charcoal, and even a chimney to take the smoke away.

- Gas barbecues are reliable and ready immediately, but charcoal is more fun, despite the wait.

- Position the barbecue where the smoke will not be a problem. Consider your guests, your neighbours and open house windows.

- Keep the barbecue away from flammable features such as plants, fences, sheds and trellis.

- Keep an eye on children.

top 5 features for guests

- Lots of comfortable chairs
- Shade
- Alfresco cooking
- Large dining table
- Pleasant atmosphere

◄ Gas barbecues take the unpredictability out of outdoor cooking, but you will need storage space to accommodate it when it is not in use.

easy water features

There are few sounds as soothing as that of moving water, and the play of light on the surface of a pool can be magical. Water also attracts wildlife, in the form of birds, bees, butterflies, dragonflies, frogs and newts, which make the area a fascinating and lively place. Whatever size or style of garden you have, there is always space for a water feature, whether it is a wall spout, bubble fountain, formal pool or wildlife pond.

Once installed, ponds need relatively little maintenance, making them useful and interesting features for the one-hour gardener. Large ponds in particular tend to look after themselves once they are established.

A pond is best sited in an open, sunny position. Avoid positioning a water feature under deciduous trees, or falling leaves will foul the water in the autumn if they are not removed. If you are planning to have a pond with a pump or fountain it is best if you can plan the water feature before the rest of the garden is complete because laying pipes and cables is disruptive. Always get a qualified electrician to install electrical cables outside.

▲ A wall spout above trickles into this pebble-filled bowl, creating an evocative gurgling and splashing sound. This feature is safe for small children as there is no standing water.

choosing a style

- Wall fountains have water flowing out of a spout in the wall into a small pool beneath, from where it is circulated, by means of a submersible pump, via a pipe back through the spout. There are many different styles, many available in kit form. They are great for courtyard gardens and are fairly safe for children.

- Bubble fountains are the safest form of water feature if there are children in the garden. Water bubbles up through a hole in a pile of cobbles, a millstone, a boulder or the top of a terracotta urn and is recycled by a pump via an underground reservoir. Many kits are available.

- Troughs, sinks and barrels are suitable for patios or small gardens. If the container is not watertight, it can be lined with a piece of butyl pond liner.

- Formal ponds are usually geometric in shape and edged with paving or bricks. They can be raised or at ground level and are usually built into a patio. Use plants to soften the edges.

- Informal ponds have an irregular shape and are designed to look like natural features. They usually have an edging of irregular stones or cobbles, with plenty of foliage around to soften the effect and help the water blend in with its surroundings.

- Streams and waterfalls must be carefully planned to be successful and made to look as natural as possible through the use of rocks, shingle and plants. They are often combined with a rock garden feature.

save time

- Plant pond plants in mesh baskets so they can easily be lifted if they need to be divided.

- Make provision for a proper edging to the pond. A loose arrangement of stones will be dangerous; weeds and grass will grow up in the gaps and be difficult to remove.

- Avoid invasive pond plants like *Typha latifolia* (bulrush), which will need constant thinning out.

- Don't put fish in the pond unless you will have the time to feed them regularly in summer if they need it. A pond should attract frogs and newts, which are just as much fun and don't need pampering.

encouraging wildlife

Ponds will attract wild animals, birds and insects to drink and bathe, so remember to give them access to the water by providing a shallow bank or pebble beach at one end. Plant some lush foliage plants both around and in the water to provide cover for shy creatures.

solar-powered pond accessories

Introducing electricity into the garden is expensive, so look around for solar-powered pumps, fountains and pool lights that, while not as powerful as their mains-powered equivalents, are safe and convenient to use. As long as you have somewhere suitable to position the solar panels, you can get a range of pumps that are capable of giving a flow of up to 1500 litres (330 gallons) per hour, sufficient to provide a continuous deep flow.

Free-floating fountains can produce a spray to 30cm (12in) high, which would be appropriate for a small pool, and floating lights, in red, yellow and green, will give up to eight hours illumination and are automatically recharged during the day.

▶ Fountains come in all shapes and sizes and create many different effects. This modern fountain has a curtain of small jets in a spiral arrangement and is enhanced by underwater lights.

care plan

- Top up the water level in warm weather, especially in a small water feature.

- Remove fallen leaves and other debris from the pond from time to time, particularly in autumn.

- Thin out oxygenating plants as soon as they start to choke the pond.

- Divide other pond plants that become rampant, cutting them back as necessary.

- Service the pond pump regularly if you've got one.

favourite plants for small ponds

Choose from among the following for your water feature. Aim to cover about half the surface of the water with foliage and make sure there is a good selection of oxygenating plants, but do not overcrowd the pond.

Aponogeton distachyos (water hawthorn)
Butomus umbellatus (flowering rush)
Caltha palustris (marsh marigold)
Hottonia palustris (water violet)
Iris laevigata
Myriophyllum aquaticum (parrot feather)
Nymphaea tetragona (dwarf waterlily)
Pistia stratiotes (water lettuce)
Pontederia cordata (pickerel weed)
Typha minima (dwarf reedmace)
Zantedeschia aethiopica (arum lily)

sitting and thinking

As in any room in the house you will need some furniture if you are to enjoy your garden to the full. There is a huge choice available in a wide range of prices from garden centres, DIY shops, junk shops and antique markets. Some is expensive, so consider carefully before you buy and be sure to try out chairs by sitting in them to test for comfort.

Choose furniture to complement the style of your garden. Some items will be permanent features that are left out all year; others can be brought out only when they are to be used. Permanent furniture must be weatherproof, so choose carefully. Take time to decide where to put it, considering whether the site is in sun or shade, in a sheltered or exposed position and whether there are scented plants or an attractive view to appreciate nearby.

If you do a lot of entertaining it is a good idea to have a few foldaway chairs for when friends come round. Deckchairs for relaxing and director's chairs for dining are always useful, provided you have somewhere to store them when they are not in use. And don't forget the simple pleasures of just sitting on a rug or blanket on the lawn.

▲ This beautiful bench with a no-nonsense design is the perfect foil for soft, full, silver planting around it.

▲ What better way to relax than to swing gently in a hammock under the dappled shade of a spreading tree?

useful options

- Dining table and chairs
- Small occasional table
- Garden bench or seat
- Steamer chairs
- Deckchairs and director's chairs
- Sunloungers
- Hammock
- Rugs or blankets for the lawn

choosing furniture ••• no care •• little care • some care

material	pros	cons
aluminium •••	Inexpensive, light and can be stylish No maintenance needed	Will not suit every garden style
hardwood •••	Low maintenance, attractive and sympathetic in all styles	Can be expensive; check that timber used comes from a renewable source
plastic •••	Inexpensive, comfortable, light and easy to move; chairs can be stacked to minimize storage space Good as a standby for guests	Doesn't always look attractive Colours may fade if left out all year
cast iron or other metals ••	Tough and durable and can be left out all year, cast aluminium doesn't rust so no maintenance required	Heavy, cast iron will rust so needs regular painting Uncomfortable to sit on for long periods
softwood •	Inexpensive and can look attractive Good for home-made furniture	Needs regular painting or preserving Cheap pieces soon become rickety
cane •	Cheap to buy, light and easy to move Looks attractive	Must be stored in a dry place
canvas or padded fabric •	Colourful, comfortable, light and very easy to move	Must be stored in a dry place when it is not in use

winter storage

Most types of furniture benefit from being stored under cover in winter, and you are unlikely to be using them at this time of year anyway. However, you need a good-sized shed or garage to accommodate a table and chairs and perhaps a sunlounger or two. If you don't have much storage space choose furniture that will tolerate winter weather or buy covers that slip over the furniture. Clean all furniture before packing it away and apply a coat of preservative to wooden items, except hardwoods. Make sure fabrics and wooden furniture are totally dry before storage or they will rot.

▶ Hardwood benches come in many different designs. They can be expensive, but you should get years of service.

let there be light

Most people have time to spend in the garden at weekends and in the evenings, and if you entertain in the garden in the evening you are likely to require some form of lighting to illuminate not only your dining area but also paths and other parts of the garden. When they are subtly lit, gardens have a magical quality that makes them seem quite different from their daytime persona.

Give as much thought to lighting as to other aspects of your garden design. Some people think that lighting their garden means flooding the entire area with a bright halogen light, but this is nearly always a mistake, for it does little to make the garden seem attractive and it is uncomfortable for anyone sitting or eating in such a glare.

Lighting should be subtle but sufficient to light paths and hazards and, if you are dining, to allow everyone to see what they are eating. What you leave unlit can be as effective as what is lit. A tree or shrub with a light shining into it takes on the appearance that it does only because of the way the shadows cast by the branches and the surrounding darkness highlight the shapes on which the light falls.

electricity

Although laying an electric cable in the garden is a large undertaking, which should be carried out only by a qualified electrician, if you are installing a submersible pump for a water feature it would be sensible to plan to use a cable from the mains for lighting right from the start. Special armoured cable should be buried in a trench about 1m (3ft) deep so that it is not accidentally damaged during normal gardening activities.

Safety regulations are being constantly tightened in the garden, and all electrical equipment must be protected by a residual current device (RCD, sometimes known as a contact circuit breaker). The trip switches in RCDs are extremely responsive, and electrical storms or power cuts often mean that they need to be reset. If your water pump or outdoor lights appear to have stopped for some reason, check that this device is not the cause. If so, it will simply require switching on again.

Lighting in the garden is increasingly being powered by the use of stepped-down, low-voltage electricity. Fortunately, low-voltage electricity is easier to install than mains voltage cable, but it does require a transformer, which steps down the mains voltage to 12 volts before it goes out into the garden. Installation is straightforward: the transformer is plugged into a power socket in the house, shed or garage and low-voltage cables lead outside to garden lights or a

◀ Garden lighting can be an attractive feature in itself. It should, however, complement the garden rather than dominate it.

pond pump. Cables do not need to be buried and can run along the surface of the soil. Do not position them across paths, where people could trip over them, nor over solid surfaces, such as rocks or paving, where the cable might be damaged.

Low-voltage lighting systems come in a wide range of styles, from bollards for illuminating paths and flights of steps to submersible lamps for ponds. They are versatile, easy and cheap to install and can be used to great effect. The main drawbacks are that they lose power the further they are positioned from the transformer – a maximum working distance of 30m (100ft) is average – and the greater the number of light fittings on each run of cable. For this reason, multiple transformers may be necessary to light a large garden effectively.

solar-powered lights

The availability, quality and range of solar-powered lights are increasing every year. The newer models have improved light levels and are more durable than the earliest versions, and some are made from aluminium. It is possible to get lights that will provide illumination for ten or more hours, although most will operate for anything between five and eight hours, with a reduced output of about three hours when light levels during the day are low.

The soft light cast by solar lighting is especially appropriate in the garden. All solar-powered lights have the advantages of being quick and easy to fit – no plugs or flexes are needed – and they can be moved around the garden as your design or needs change. They are also, of course, perfectly safe, because they are low voltage and need no mains wiring. Above all, they are environmentally friendly and completely free to operate.

The range of styles has increased in recent years, and it is now possible to get wall-mounted lights, which are suitable for illuminating entrances and doorways, ground-spike models, which can be inserted along paths or in flowerbeds and borders, and post-mounted lights for providing light at higher levels. One drawback is that, generally, once they come on, they stay on, which can be annoying.

other lights

- Candles are the simplest solution for outdoor lighting, and they create a soft, flattering light. Place candles in lanterns or jars so that they are not blown out by breezes. Buy special candles impregnated with oil of citronella, which will help keep insects and midges at bay.

- Paraffin lamps are brighter than candles and burn for longer. Hang from pergolas or trees.

- Garden flares, which are like enormous candles, are good for parties and can be positioned anywhere in the garden. Some contain an insect repellent.

▲ Garden flares are perfect for parties and barbecues as they provide a temporary source of light and an exciting atmosphere.

maintain it

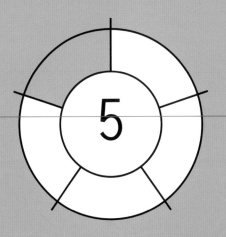

You should not, if you have followed the advice for planning and creating an easy-care garden earlier in the book, have too much work to do to keep your garden in good shape. If you have included a good selection of easy-care and no-care plants and if you have adopted low-maintenance solutions to the basic layout and design, you should have no difficulty in keeping on top of your garden in the time you have allowed yourself.

Remember that your garden has been planned for a small amount of regular maintenance. If you get out of the routine of doing little often, the work will begin to mount up, and it can be difficult to get on top of things again. If weeds are not plucked out of the borders whenever you notice them, they will be more difficult to remove and might set seed, multiplying your problems in a moment. A few moments spent removing the weeds that have popped up in the previous week will save many hours of work later on. Similarly, keeping an eye out for pests and diseases and taking early action to eliminate them will save much time and trouble when they have become established.

The more thoroughly you have prepared the garden, the less likely it is that anything will go wrong, so if you have thought about the labour-saving aspects of all the elements in your garden, you really will be able to spend just one hour a week in keeping it looking as beautiful as it was when you first finished planning it.

'the more thoroughly you have prepared the garden, the less likely it is that anything will go wrong'

◄ This spectacular border is carefully planted so that weeds cannot find room to grow and the plants that do need some maintenance are within easy reach of the path.

▲ The ultimate in easy-care gardening: a stylish patio with just
two sempervivums in the central cobbles and surrounded by
easy-care shrubs and perennials.

minimizing chores

No garden is completely maintenance free, but with a little careful thought and some organization the main chores – feeding and watering, cutting back and planting – will fit into your weekly garden hour.

a good start

Taking a little trouble at planting time will get your plants off to a good start so that they stay healthy. Prepare the ground thoroughly, removing the roots of perennial weeds and digging it over well to a depth of 30–60cm (1–2ft) depending on the size of the plants that you are putting in. Incorporate plenty of organic matter in the form of well-rotted garden compost, leaf mould or manure. This will improve any type of soil: it both opens up heavy soils to prevent waterlogging and root rot in winter and helps sandy soils to hold moisture and nutrients.

When you have prepared the soil, dig a planting hole large enough to accommodate the rootball of the plant and sprinkle a little general-purpose fertilizer in the bottom. Position the rootball in the hole so that the top is at ground level and backfill the hole with soil. Firm the soil well around the rootball and water well. Repeat the process with any other plants you are planting, and then mulch the surface of the soil to retain moisture and suppress weeds.

▲ Plants should be arranged relatively close together so there is no space between them for weeds to get established. This also helps to keep the soil moist.

fail-safe feeding

Feeding is vital for keeping plants healthy and free from problems. Plants, especially those growing in a border, will not shrivel up and die if you forget to feed them regularly, but they will become increasingly weak and prone to attack from pests and diseases, which will take time and effort to sort out, and in the worst cases could mean that you have to dig the plants up and start again.

Shrubs, trees and established perennials will manage happily on just one feed a year. Apply slow-release fertilizer pellets or granules in spring, forking them lightly into the soil around the plant. You can do the same with permanent container displays.

Herbs, vegetables and bedding plants will need more frequent feeding as they grow so fast. Use a fast-acting liquid feed regularly throughout the growing season. Liquid feeds are diluted in water and applied to the soil when you water. Take time to read the packaging before you buy fertilizers to check you are getting the right product for the plants you want to feed, and always follow the manufacturer's instructions about dilution and frequency.

Choose organic products if you can. Chemical fertilizers can scorch plant roots if they are not applied properly, and organic products create a much more natural balance of nutrients in the soil.

watering tips

If you mulch beds and borders in spring when the soil is moist, you shouldn't need to water established shrubs and perennials except during periods of prolonged and severe drought. However, you will need to water newly planted plants for about a year after planting, until they are well established. Containers and edibles will also need watering regularly throughout the year.

● Water thoroughly and infrequently to encourage plants to grow deep roots. If you just wet the surface of the soil, plants develop shallow roots that are more vulnerable to drought.

● Don't try to water everything in dry weather unless you have the time to do it well. It is better to concentrate your efforts on vulnerable plants and water these thoroughly.

● Stand containers in saucers in dry weather and mulch the top of the compost. For other container watering tips, see pages 96–7.

● Keep a close eye on new plants for about a year after planting. They will be vulnerable to drought until they are well established.

● Water edibles such as vegetables and salad crops frequently to ensure a good crop.

cutting back

Herbaceous perennials – both flowering and foliage plants – die back in late autumn each year to re-emerge fresh each spring. The dead foliage has to be cleared away to make way for the new growth, and this can be done in the autumn after flowering or early the following spring.

The advantages of tidying up in spring are that the old vegetation protects the crown of the plant from penetrating frosts and provides a home for insects on which birds can feed. The disadvantages are that it is all too easy to damage emerging shoots if you leave the cutting back too late and the dead foliage and stems may overwinter pests and diseases. Your decision will depend on the micro-climate in your garden and on whether you find frost-touched dead stems and seedheads attractive.

▶ Large containers need far less regular watering than small ones, but still need to be checked frequently in warm weather.

organizing the workload

Some people really enjoy the annual round of digging, weeding, pruning and propagating that constitutes traditional gardening, but for most of us these days, gardening is a means to an end – the process by which we achieve an attractive place to relax outside – and as such we do the minimum to get what we want. As we have shown, it is possible to reduce the chores to almost nothing, but you would have to make some fairly sweeping design changes to do this. Most people end up with a garden that needs a little care and attention to keep it looking good, and when the pressure's off and you don't really have that much to do outside, it can become quite enjoyable and relaxing. The golden rule for keeping on top of the low-maintenance garden is to do little and often.

avoiding trouble

- Plant properly after good soil preparation to give plants a good start (see page 124).

- Keep borders tidy – remove dead foliage and rotting leaves so they don't harbour diseases or pests, such as slugs and snails.

- Keep plants healthy by regular feeding and care. Weak plants are more prone to disease and pest attack than strong, healthy ones.

- Choose easy-care plants to avoid unnecessary pruning, spraying or cosseting.

- Make sure that you pick the right plants for the position so they will thrive and stay healthy.

- Buy good-quality, vigorous stock.

- Keep the weeds down by regular weeding. Smaller weeds are much easier to remove than those that have become established.

planning your time

If you follow all the points above to avoid trouble, you shouldn't have too much to cope with.

- Follow the self-organizer on pages 148–57 to show you what you should be doing when. The times taken to do individual tasks will, of course, vary from garden to garden and, in any case, bad weather will prevent you getting out some weekends, but you should be able to plan ahead so that you know what tasks you should be doing each week.

- Do a job as soon as it needs doing: it will only get worse with time and will take you longer when you do get round to doing it.

- Deal with pests and diseases as soon as you notice them (see pages 136–7).

- Only do a job when the conditions are suitable. For example, it is best to avoid standing on the soil when it is very wet as you will compact it badly, so put off cutting back or planting until the soil dries a little. Likewise, avoid planting out new plants in frosty, very dry or very cold weather, and don't start mowing the lawn until the weather warms and the grass begins to grow.

- Be flexible with timings when you have to be.

◄ Keeping weeds under control before they become established should ensure that you don't have to spend hours trying to get rid of them later in the summer.

▲ Deadheading roses need take only a few minutes a week. Simple routine maintenance of this kind only becomes a major chore if left to build up over a long period.

time-saving tools and equipment

Using the right equipment will make your gardening easier and less of a chore. You will not need a vast range of tools to maintain an easy-care garden, although you will need a wider selection for the initial work involved in transforming the garden in the first place. Consider hiring these if you will have no further use for them after the preparatory work.

Always buy the best quality tools you can afford, because they will more than pay for themselves in the long run. Look after them by keeping them clean, sharp and oiled to lengthen their useful lives. Store them in a dry place, and if necessary keep them where they can be locked away, to keep them safe from children and burglars.

gardening tools

- Spade: essential for planting, digging over uncultivated soil and applying mulches to borders. Stainless steel is the best and longest lasting, but also the most expensive. They are available in different heights and with different handles, so choose one that is comfortable to hold.

- Fork: invaluable for breaking up soil and incorporating organic matter. Choose a lightweight fork that will be easy to use and make sure it is the right height so that you do not strain your back.

- Trowel: indispensable for planting small plants and bulbs and for removing small weeds. Stainless steel is the best. Buy one that feels comfortable in your hand and is well balanced.

- Hand fork: ideal for loosening the soil and weeding between plants. Choose a fork with flat tines if possible. Again, stainless steel is worth the investment.

- Hoe: useful but not vital for lightweight weeding without bending down. Several designs are available, so try them out before you buy to see which you prefer.

- Secateurs: essential for pruning and deadheading. Buy the best you can afford. Anvil secateurs have a sharp blade that cuts down on to a flat edge, while scissor types have a sharp blade that cuts against another, thicker blade. Anvil secateurs are usually easier to use but leave a ragged edge and don't last as long. Ratchet secateurs are available for those with weaker hands. Make sure you buy secateurs that are comfortable to hold. Left-handed models are available and are worth seeking out if you find that the normal type is difficult to operate.

▲ A spring-tine rake is one of the few essential tools that you need in the garden—it will make quick work of leaves in autumn without ruining the grass underneath.

- Wheelbarrow: useful for collecting weeds and prunings and for moving mulch or new plants to borders. Don't get too big a barrow if you have a small garden, especially as you will have to find somewhere to store it.

- Garden hose: useful, even if you only have a very small garden, for watering plants and containers. A hose is far less time consuming and back-breaking than constantly refilling a watering can. If you don't have much space, some hoses wind flat on to a small cartridge for storage. Fit an outside tap for added convenience.

- Long-armed loppers: necessary for making light work of pruning larger stems and invaluable if you have a lot of trees and shrubs. Loppers with a geared action are especially useful.

- Lawnmower: necessary only if you have a lawn. Whether you choose a hover or a rotary mower, for the one-hour garden a model with a grass collection box is essential.

- Hedge-trimmers: essential if you have a hedge of any size, although you could get away with shears for a small hedge. Choose electric trimmers with an extension lead; petrol-driven trimmers can be quite heavy and noisy.

- Gloves and goggles: protect yourself in the garden. Choose thin gloves for light work so you can feel what you are doing and move your fingers without restriction and heavy-duty gloves for spiny shrubs. Wear goggles when you are using a hedge-trimmer or a strimmer.

- Broom: useful for sweeping up fallen leaves, but is only necessary if there are a lot of deciduous trees and shrubs in and around your garden.

- Rake: ideal for raking up leaves, levelling soil after digging and raking over gravel and bark chips. A spring-tine rake is useful for scarifying a small lawn.

▲ A small tool store is perfect for an easy-care garden. Some come in chest form, others can be attached to a wall.

essential tools

Even in the smallest low-maintenance garden you will need:

- Secateurs ● Hand fork ● Trowel

- Spade ● Fork

A wheelbarrow is useful but not essential (and you need somewhere to keep it) and a garden hose is essential for topping up anything but the smallest of ponds.

controlling weeds

Of all gardening tasks, weeding is one of the most time consuming, recurring and dull. Areas of bare soil between plants will be an invitation for annual and perennial weeds to take hold, and, as in most aspects of low-maintenance gardening, prevention is better than cure. Covering all bare soil with a mulch is by far the best approach to weed control. The mulch will prevent weed seeds germinating, and, because it will help to retain moisture in the soil below, it will help your chosen plants to grow strongly and healthily, so that they spread and, in turn, prevent weeds from taking hold.

There are three main types of mulch: organic, weed-suppressing and living. Organic mulches include well-rotted garden compost, rotted manure or leaf mould. These will gradually be incorporated into the soil through the action of worms and will need topping up each year, but they do help to improve the soil and benefit the plants. In late spring each year remove all weeds from the border and add a layer of mulch to a depth of 5–8cm (2–3in) to cover the surface of the soil, taking care that you do not pack it around the plant stems. If new weeds seed themselves in the mulch they will be easy to pull out by hand.

Weed-suppressing mulches, such as gravel or bark chippings, should be laid over a semi-permeable membrane to be most effective. This is usually thick black polythene sheeting, woven polypropylene which allows rainwater to be absorbed into the soil, or woven black plastic sheeting, which is resilient. The membrane prevents perennial weeds from growing altogether, and any annual weed seeds that do germinate in the mulch can be quickly removed because they cannot get their roots into the soil.

Living mulches are carpet-forming groundcover plants growing together to cover the soil with a dense mat of foliage that prevents weed seeds germinating. See pages 84–5 for some suggestions on suitable plants to use.

Use chemical weedkillers only when you really have to. If you are faced with an overgrown and neglected garden, you may want to use chemicals to clear the ground before you begin. Read the instructions carefully to make sure you are buying the right product and follow them to the letter when using it. Gardeners who try to avoid chemicals altogether will prefer to rid the soil of weeds by fastening sheets of black polythene over the surface of the soil and leaving it for several months.

It is possible to buy ready-mixed weedkillers in hand sprayers to use in a restricted area – they are quick and convenient – but do not use sprays of any kind in windy weather or you will find that the spray drifts on to other, wanted plants.

◀ It is worth spending a little time each week getting rid of weeds when they are small—the bigger they grow, the more difficult their roots will be to remove.

easy weed control

- Apply a mulch to beds and borders every spring to stop weeds germinating. Any weeds that do appear will be easy to remove. A mulch also improves soil condition and retains moisture.

- Use a weed-suppressing membrane where possible.

- Plant close together to keep the soil covered and to stop weeds germinating.

- Avoid digging over the soil as it will bring up new weed seeds. Lightly fork over the surface when necessary and add a mulch in spring.

- Remove weeds as soon as they appear, especially if they are growing among border plants.

- Remove perennial weed roots as soon and as thoroughly as possible. If you leave the smallest piece of the root of stinging nettles, bindweed or ground elder, for example, it will soon regrow.

- Remove annual weeds before they set seed.

▲ Gravel mulch is an effective weed suppressant when laid over a semi-permeable membrane. The membrane stops weeds coming through while allowing water to be absorbed.

keeping the lawn looking good

If you have decided that a lawn will be a useful and attractive feature in your garden, it will need regular attention to keep it healthy and vigorous. However, there are plenty of steps you can take to minimize the amount of time you need to spend on keeping your lawn in good condition.

golden rules for easy-care lawns

- Don't allow plants to spill out of the borders on to the lawn. This makes mowing virtually impossible and leaves nasty bald patches that will need attention later on.

- Keep the lawn shape simple to make mowing quicker and easier. Fiddly corners and small borders cut into it will make the job tedious.

- Create a proper edging to the lawn (see below).

- Avoid lawns in shady sites. The grass will not thrive, so rather than embark on an uphill struggle, try another surface instead.

save time

- Remove features, such as seats, containers, trees, island beds and birdbaths, that you will have to mow round.

- Smooth out sharp corners and fussy tight curves – broad, sweeping shapes will greatly reduce mowing time.

- Make sure there are no low branches on nearby trees that you will have to duck under.

- Avoid narrow areas of lawn, less than about 1m (3ft) across, which concentrate the wear on the grass and cause bald patches, which will require relaying or reseeding.

- Use paving slabs for paths and entrances or sink stepping stones into the lawn.

- Don't plant bulbs in the lawn, unless it's in an area of rough grass or meadow that you mow infrequently because you cannot mow over bulb foliage for at least six weeks after flowering.

▲ Set stepping stones below the level of the lawn so you can simply run the mower over the top of them.

edging

Edging helps to define the shape of the lawn and also cuts down on the ghastly and totally unnecessary job of clipping the edges of the grass. Set the edging just below the level of the lawn to allow the mower to pass over it without damage to either. An edging strip can be a feature in its own right. Integrate it into the overall garden design by co-ordinating the materials with the patio or other areas of hard landscaping. If the edging is wide enough, allow some of the border plants to spill on to it to create an exuberant effect without ruining the lawn.

easy-care lawn programme

- Mowing – Regular mowing not only makes the lawn easier to walk on but also creates a dense sward that stops weeds growing.

- Removing autumn leaves – Sweeping up leaves as they fall will stop the grass from becoming dry and prevent bald patches forming.

- Watering – Drought rarely actually kills a lawn. Although the grass will become brown and unsightly it soon gets back its colour after some rain. If you do decide to water your lawn in warm weather, water it very thoroughly to encourage deep roots to form. Moistening the surface will cause the grass to grow shallow roots, making it even more vulnerable to drought. A sprinkler attached to a hose is the only practicable method.

- Feeding – Apply a lawn feed each spring when the grass starts into active growth. Granular or powered products are easiest to apply, and you could make life easy by hiring a special distributor for large lawns. If the lawn is weedy, use a combined weed and feed product.

▶ This brick path acts as a mowing strip between lawn and flowerbed, making lawn edge trimming unnecessary.

lawn care calendar

spring

Start mowing in early or mid-spring when the soil is fairly dry and the grass has started to grow.

For the first few cuts set the mower blades quite high – e.g., 4–5cm (1½–2in).

Cut once a week or fortnightly, depending on grass growth.

Apply a granular or powdered lawn feed in mid- or late spring.

summer

Cut the grass once a week while it is growing well.

Keep it down to about 2.5cm (1in) to encourage sideways growth to thicken the lawn.

If the weather is dry, cut the grass fortnightly and raise the mowing height to 4cm (1½in).

autumn

Mow fortnightly until mid-autumn when the grass growth starts to slow down.

Rake or sweep fallen leaves off the lawn.

winter

No lawn care is particularly necessary, although you can mow the lawn from time to time if it is not too wet or frosty and you want to keep it neat.

basic pruning

▲ Reduce the size of evergreen shrubs such as camellias by cutting them back in late spring. Cut each stem down to just above a leaf joint.

Pruning is probably the one job that most instils fear into inexperienced gardeners, but there is no reason why it should, and if you have chosen from the easy-care plants listed on pages 140–45 you will need to do only a minimal amount of pruning anyway.

why prune?

There are three main reasons for pruning:

- To reduce the size of the shrub or tree if it is outgrowing its space.

- To keep a plant healthy by removing dead or diseased branches.

- To maintain the flowering or fruiting performance of the plant.

Most shrubs respond well to an annual prune, which should usually be done soon after flowering, but it is not absolutely necessary in the majority of cases. You may get slightly fewer and smaller flowers if you don't prune, but for most of us that is not a problem. A few shrubs do need to be pruned each year or they soon become leggy and shy to flower. Only a few plants mentioned in the book need this type of pruning. This would normally preclude plants as being classed as easy-care, but it would be a shame to leave out shrubs such as *Buddleja davidii* (butterfly bush) when cutting back is so straightforward, and in every other sense it is really is an easy-care plant.

trouble-free pruning

There is nothing mysterious about pruning.

- Use sharp secateurs for small shrubs, and keep them sharpened for easier use. Buy the best quality you can afford: they will be easier to use and last so much longer that you will save money in the long run.

- Long-armed loppers make easy work of tall plants and thicker stems. Choose a pair with 'gearing' to take most of the effort out of cutting.

- Make the cuts as clean as possible and afterwards use a sharp knife to pare away any ragged edges that could harbour disease.

- Use a pruning saw to branches from small tree. Cut as close to the main stem as possible so you do not leave a stump. Start by cutting about quarter of the way up through the branch from underneath, cut down from above to join up and sever the branch neatly.

pruning plan

The golden rule is to prune soon after flowering. Each branch on most shrubs will flower only once, so when it has flowered it may as well be removed. This encourages new shoots to form and gives them a year to grow and mature before they, in turn, produce flowers.

The exceptions are those shrubs that flower in early autumn, such as *Buddleja davidii* (butterfly bush). If they are pruned immediately after flowering the new shoots that formed would be vulnerable to winter frosts, so it is better to leave the pruning until the spring.

If you are in any doubt, do not prune.

▶ Prune *Viburnum tinus* after it has flowered in late spring. This will help to keep it in shape and promote bushy growth on which the following year's flowers will form.

pruning at a glance

plant type	timing	action
Deciduous shrubs that flower before late spring	Prune straight after flowering	Cut back the branches that have flowered, remove any weak or crowded stems
Deciduous shrubs that flower after late spring	Prune in late winter or early spring	Cut back some of the stems to the ground, remove dead, weak or overcrowded branches
Evergreen shrubs	Prune in late spring if necessary	Cut out weak or overcrowded branches

pests and diseases

No matter how healthy the plants and how tidy the garden, you will encounter unwelcome pests and diseases from time to time. Deal with problems as soon as they arise so that they do not get out of hand.

You will be unfortunate if you encounter more than a few more common pests and diseases, especially if you stick to the easy-care plants in the directory and avoid growing a lot of vegetables. The following pests and diseases might need treatment; other problems can damage flowers and leaves but do not usually present a serious threat to plants.

◄ Leaves affected by rust should be removed.

common plant pests: easy identifier

pest	symptoms	treatment
aphids (including greenfly and blackfly)	Colonies of tiny green, black or pink insects (sometimes other colours), clinging to stems and sucking the sap, causing distortion and inhibiting growth	Remove small outbreaks by hand, apply an insecticidal soap, use a selective insecticide (such as pirimicarb), encourage natural predators (blue tits, ladybirds and hoverflies) into your garden
earwigs	Young leaves and flowers eaten at night	Trap earwigs in upturned flowerpots filled with straw pushed onto canes inserted into the soil among susceptible plants so that they can be removed each morning and destroyed
scale insects	Small, immobile, brown or yellowish insects, resembling tiny blisters on stems and the undersides of leaves, suck the sap and weaken growth	Remove with a damp cloth if possible. Use an insecticidal spray (such as malathion). If plants are susceptible to scale insects, apply a non-dry glue to stems to prevent the larvae climbing up the plant; in greenhouses use a parasitic wasp (*Metaphycus helvolus*)
slugs and snails	Leaves and sometimes entire plants stripped overnight, slime trails often visible	Saucers of beer or upturned orange skins among plants attract slugs and snails, which can be removed and discarded each morning. Use 'safe' slug pellets that do not harm wildlife or pets and can be used around edible plants. Water in nematodes (*Phasmarhabditis hermaphrodita*)
vine weevils	Leaves have U-shaped holes in edges (made by adult beetle) or the entire plant collapses and dies because larvae (small, C-shaped grubs) eat root systems	Use non-stick glue around containers. Water in nematodes (*Heterorhabditis megidis* or *Steinernema carpocapsae*) in late summer or autumn

common plant problems: easy identifier

disease	symptoms	treatment
grey mould (also known as botrytis)	Patches of fluffy, grey mould appear on stems, leaves and flowers, particularly in damp weather	Cut out and burn affected stems in autumn. Spray with a suitable fungicide (such as carbendazim). Avoid poor drainage, overwatering and overcrowding
mosaic virus	Yellow leaves, twisted stems and misshapen flowers	Remove and burn all infected plants straight away to stop it spreading
powdery mildew	Powdery, white patches on leaves, stems and flowers, often seen in hot, dry weather	Keep plants well watered and mulched. Cut out affected stems in autumn. Spray with a fungicide (such as mancozeb)
rust	Brown or orange pustules on the undersides of leaves	Remove affected leaves and apply a potash fertilizer. If roses are affected apply a systemic fungicide (such as mancozeb)
silver leaf	Leaves of trees and shrubs (especially *Prunus* spp.) turn silvery then brown; eventually entire branches die back	Remove and burn all affected branches, cutting back until the brown staining is no longer visible in the wood. Remove and burn badly affected plants
sooty mould	Black or dark brown mould on leaf surfaces growing on honeydew, a sticky substance deposited by some insects	Wash off the mould if it bothers you; use a systemic insecticide to combat the insects producing the honeydew

avoiding trouble

One of the keys to easy-care gardening is to prevent trouble before it happens. Make sure that you avoid problems before they can become time consuming and difficult to eradicate:

- Buy problem-free plants (see pages 140–47).

- Deal with a problem as soon as you see it.

- Keep the garden tidy and do not leave dead plant matter, old flowerpots or boxes around that might harbour diseases or pests.

- Keep plants healthy by regular watering and feeding to help them fight disease and pest attack.

- If a plant dies examine it and the soil around it for signs of pests or diseases that might move to other plants.

- Encourage birds into the garden by providing a bird feeder and water for them. They will feed on aphids and other insect pests, keeping the numbers down.

keep it simple

Don't try to kill everything in sight. Most garden insects are actually beneficial, killing the pests that do harm.

Try non-chemical controls before you resort to spraying with chemicals. Aphids, for example, can be removed with a jet of water from a garden hose or washed off with soapy water. Slugs and snails can be caught in beer traps or under orange or grapefruit skins. There is also an increasing range of organic products available. Watering nematodes into the garden and into your containers once or twice a year is not difficult and does not take much time.

Use chemicals only when you have to and always follow the manufacturer's instructions, especially those relating to dilution, frequency and safety. There is a huge selection of pesticides and fungicides on offer, and they contain different ingredients and work in different ways. Read the information carefully before you buy to make sure the product you choose is suitable. Also check whether it is safe near children, pets and edible plants. If in doubt, ask the supplier.

easy propagation

The easiest way to acquire new plants is to get them from family and friends. After that, for speed and convenience, buying from garden centres or the gardening departments of large DIY stores is far the best solution. However, while most of us do not have the time, know-how or inclination to raise all our plants from seeds or cuttings, there are a few really easy ways to get new plants and to save some money at the same time.

sowing seeds

Most garden plants can be grown from seed, but it is the hardy annuals – those summer-flowering annuals that can be sown straight into the ground – that are the easiest to grow. They include *Centaurea cyanus* (cornflower), *Nigella damascena* (love-in-a-mist), *Calendula officinalis* (pot marigold), *Eschscholzia californica* (California poppy) and *Tropaeolum majus* (nasturtium). They are great for filling gaps in borders. All you need do is sow in late spring and wait for the show of flowers. Here's how:

1 Fork over the soil lightly in late spring to produce a fine crumb. Draw the edge of a trowel or hand fork across the soil to make a number of parallel shallow drills, about 20cm (8in) apart.

2 Sprinkle the seeds thinly in the drills and cover them over with a fine sprinkling of soil. Sowing in drills means that you will know which of the emerging plants are seedlings and which are weeds.

3 Water the patch thoroughly and keep the soil moist as the seeds germinate and grow. If the seedlings come up too thickly pull some of them out to give the others more room.

▲ If you want an early show of annuals in the garden, you can sow seed in trays indoors rather than waiting until it is warm enough to sow them out of doors.

dividing perennials

Most herbaceous perennials can be increased by simply digging them up, splitting them into a number of smaller pieces and replanting them. The new divisions will quickly spread to form large clumps themselves. This is a great way to get new plants, but it is also good for the plants, because in the process the old, weak growth is removed, giving the stronger, new growth more space to spread.

Division can be done any time from late autumn to spring, but it is easiest in mid-spring because you will be able to see what you are doing more clearly as the new shoots are emerging. This is all you need do:

1 Dig up the clump and remove most of the soil around the roots so you can see what you are doing.

2 Split the clump into smaller, healthy sections, discarding any dead or weak growth in the middle of the clump. Depending on the plant, you may be able to do this with your hands, but sometimes you will have to use a sharp knife to separate the sections. To divide really large clumps, insert two garden forks, back to back, into the clump and bring the handles together to force the tines apart and separate the roots.

3 Make sure that each division has some roots and some top growth. Prepare the soil and replant the sections. Fork in some slow-release fertilizer, firm the soil back around the roots and water well. Keep moist until the plants are well established.

▶ Polyanthus are easy to divide as the clumps are made up of a number of distinct crowns that pull apart quite simply.

layering

One of the easiest of all methods of propagating shrubs is to the layer them. This is the cheat's version of taking cuttings, but works only on shrubs that have flexible branches that will reach down to the ground.

1 Bend down the branch to the ground and mark the point where it touches the soil.

2 Make a small trench at this point and fill it with a handful of potting compost and grit mixed together.

3 Make a small cut in the bottom of the branch, about a third of the way through, where it touches the compost. Twist the branch slightly to open up the cut but make sure you do not detach the branch from the parent plant.

4 Lay the cut branch on the gritty compost, cover with a little more compost and place a heavy stone on top of the branch to hold it in place.

5 Between six and nine months later roots should have formed in the cut. Detach the branch from the parent plant and pot it up or plant it elsewhere. Water it well and keep it moist until established.

plants-at-a-glance

One of the main aspects of creating an easy-care garden is to choose plants that look after themselves and do most of the hard work for you. The plants listed on the following pages are those that have been used in the planting schemes described elsewhere in this book. They were chosen because they are widely available and require little attention: they are hardy, reliable and need little if any pruning or cutting back.

The plants are grouped as trees, climbers, shrubs, perennials and hardy annuals, plants grown for their foliage and bulbs, corms and tubers. The height and spread indicated are those likely to be attained ultimately by plants grown in good soil in optimum conditions.

trees

	height / spread	special features	care plan
Betula utilis var. *jacquemontii* (Himalayan birch)	18 x 10m (60 x 30ft)	Deciduous, with stunning white bark and delicate foliage	Sun/partial shade, moist/normal soil. Prune in summer if necessary
Crataegus laevigata 'Paul's Scarlet' (hawthorn)	8 x 8m (25 x 25ft)	Deciduous, with rich pink flowers in spring and red berries	Sun/partial shade, moist/normal/dry soil. Prune after flowering if necessary or after leaf-fall if used for hedging
Ilex x altaclerensis 'Golden King' (holly)	6 x 6m (20 x 20ft)	Evergreen, smooth-edged leaves with yellow margins, red berries, good for hedges	Sun/partial shade, moist/normal soil. Prune in winter or midsummer if necessary
Juniperus communis 'Compressa' (common juniper)	80 x 45cm (32 x 18in)	Evergreen. Neat, slow growing, column-shaped conifer	Sun/partial shade, normal/dry soil. Prune in spring or autumn if necessary
Malus x zumi 'Golden Hornet' (crabapple)	10 x 8m (30 x 25ft)	Deciduous, with white blossom in spring and golden-yellow crabapples	Sun/partial shade, moist/normal soil. Remove dead and diseased branches in winter
Prunus serrula (ornamental cherry/birch bark tree)	10 x 10m (30 x 30ft)	Deciduous, with glossy, coppery bark, white blossom in spring and cherry-like fruits	Sun, moist/normal soil. Cut back in midsummer if necessary
Salix caprea 'Kilmarnock' (Kilmarnock willow)	1.5 x 2m (5 x 6ft)	Deciduous, with an attractive weeping shape and catkins in spring	Sun, moist/normal soil. Trim lightly in late winter or early spring only if necessary
Sorbus aria 'Lutescens' (whitebeam)	10 x 8m (30 x 25ft)	Deciduous, with silvery foliage, white flowers in spring and red berries	Sun/partial shade, normal/dry soil. No pruning required

climbers

	height	special features	care plan
Clematis montana var. *rubens* '**Tetrarose**'	5–8m (15–25ft)	Deciduous, with purple-green leaves and pink flowers in spring	Sun/partial shade, normal soil. Grow with roots in shade and prune after flowering
Hedera helix (common ivy)	varies	Evergreen, with many decorative leaf shapes, colours and variegations. Good groundcover	Sun/partial shade/shade, moist/normal/dry soil (thrives in poor soil). Prune in spring and pull up out-of-place runners at any time
Humulus lupulus '**Aureus**' (golden hop)	6m (20ft)	Deciduous, with golden-yellow foliage and hops in summer	Sun/partial shade, moist/normal soil. Clear away dead growth in autumn or early spring
Lonicera periclymenum (honeysuckle)	7m (22ft)	Deciduous, with fragrant white or yellow flowers in summer, followed by red berries	Sun/partial shade, moist/normal soil. Cut back straggly stems in autumn or spring
Parthenocissus quinquefolia (Virginia creeper)	15m (50ft)	Deciduous, with attractive foliage turning bright red in autumn. Good cover for walls	Sun/partial shade/shade, normal/dry soil. Remove unwanted stems in summer

◄ (top left) *Crataegus laevigata* 'Rosea Flore Pleno' (hawthorn) has profuse flowers in spring, followed by red berries.
▲ *Humulus lupulus* 'Aureus' is a twining perennial climber with attractive, golden-yellow foliage as well as greenish yellow flowers (hops) in autumn.
► *Clematis montana* var. *rubens* grows into a large plant that is literally covered in blooms in late spring.

deciduous shrubs

	height/spread	special features	care plan
Berberis thunbergii	1.5 x 2m (5 x 6ft)	Colourful autumn foliage and small red berries	Sun, moist/normal soil. Prune in late winter if necessary
Buddleja davidii (butterfly bush)	3 x 5m (10 x15ft)	Dense heads of purple flowers in summer. Attracts butterflies	Sun, normal/dry soil. Cut back all stems to 30cm (12in) in early spring
Chaenomeles superba (flowering quince)	1.5 x 2m (5 x 6ft)	Exotic flowers spring to summer followed by green fruits	Sun/partial shade, normal/dry soil. Cut back after flowering if necessary
Cotinus coggygria (smoke bush)	5 x 5m (15 x 15ft)	Purple or wine-red foliage	Sun/partial shade, moist/normal soil. Cut back hard in early spring for large, well-coloured leaves
Cotoneaster horizontalis (fishbone cotoneaster)	1 x 1.5m (3 x 5ft)	Stems form unusual herring-bone pattern. White flowers and red berries	Sun/partial shade, normal/dry soil. Prune in late winter if necessary
Genista lydia (broom)	0.6 x 1m (2 x 3ft)	Masses of yellow flowers in early summer and a nice arching habit	Sun, normal/dry soil. Prune in late winter but do not cut into old wood
Hamamelis x intermedia (witch hazel)	4 x 4m (12 x 12ft)	Fragrant yellow or orange flowers in winter and autumn foliage colour	Sun/partial shade, moist/normal soil. Remove dead and damaged branches in late winter or early spring
Hydrangea macrophylla	2 x 2.5m (6 x 8ft)	Large flowerheads in white, pink or blue in summer	Sun/partial shade/shade, moist/normal soil. Cut off dead flowers. Prune in early spring
Jasminum nudiflorum (winter jasmine)	3 x 3m (10 x 10ft)	Yellow flowers in winter	Sun/partial shade, normal soil. Cut back flowered stems after flowering
Lavatera 'Barnsley' (mallow)	2 x 2m (6 x 6ft)	Large pale pink flowers in summer. Sometimes semi-evergreen	Sun/partial shade, normal/dry soil. Cut back all stems to 30cm (12in) in early spring
Potentilla fruticosa (cinquefoil)	1.2 x 1.2m (4 x 4ft)	Red, pink, yellow or white flowers from late spring to autumn	Sun, normal/dry soil. Prune after flowering if necessary
Ribes sanguineum (flowering currant)	2 x 2m (6 x 6ft)	Clusters of pink flowers in spring. Good for hedges	Sun/partial shade, normal/dry soil. Prune after flowering
Rosa rugosa (hedgehog rose)	2 x 2m (6 x 6ft)	Large pink flowers from summer to autumn and large red hips. Good for hedges	Sun/partial shade, moist/normal soil. Prune in spring
Spiraea japonica 'Shirobana'	60 x 60cm (2 x 2ft)	Dark pink and white flowers together in summer	Sun, moist/normal soil. Cut back hard in early spring
Viburnum plicatum 'Mariesii' (Japanese snowball bush)	3 x 4m (10 x 12ft)	Branches form layered effect. White flowers in spring and good autumn colour	Sun/partial shade, moist/normal soil. Cut out old wood in early spring

evergreen shrubs

	height/spread	special features	care plan
Aucuba japonica **'Crotonifolia'** (spotted laurel)	3 x 3m (10 x 10ft)	Glossy leaves spotted with yellow. Red berries in autumn	Sun/partial shade/shade. Moist/normal/dry soil (thrives in poor soil). Cut out any all-green shoots
Berberis x *stenophylla* (barberry)	3 x 5m (10 x 15ft)	Yellow-orange flowers in spring. Good for hedges	Sun/partial shade, normal/dry soil. Trim hedges after flowering
Choisya ternata (Mexican orange blossom)	2.5 x 2.5m (8 x 8ft)	Glossy leaves, and fragrant white flowers in spring and summer	Sun, normal/dry soil. Protect from cold, drying winds. No pruning required
Elaeagnus pungens **'Maculata'**	4 x 5m (12 x 15ft)	Glossy green leaves with bold yellow centres and red berries. Makes a good hedge	Sun/partial shade, normal/dry soil. Cut out any all-green shoots
Erica carnea (heather)	25 x 60cm (10 x 24in)	Purple or pink flowers from winter to spring	Sun/partial shade, normal soil. Shear over immediately after flowering
Euonymus fortunei **'Emerald 'n' Gold'**	0.6 x 1m (2 x 3ft)	Glossy green and yellow foliage, tinged pink in winter	Sun/partial shade, normal/dry soil (thrives in poor soil). Cut out all-green shoots. Prune in mid-spring if necessary
Fatsia japonica (Japanese aralia)	3 x 3m (10 x 10ft)	Large, glossy, hand-shaped leaves, white flowers in autumn followed by black fruits. Architectural form	Sun/partial shade/shade, moist/normal soil. No pruning required
Hypericum calycinum (rose of Sharon)	60cm (2ft) x indefinite	May be semi-evergreen. Large yellow flowers summer to autumn. Good groundcover	Sun/partial shade/shade, oist/normal soil (thrives in poor soil). Cut back in early spring
Lavandula angustifolia **'Hidcote'** (lavender)	60 x 75cm (24 x 30in)	Silvery foliage, purple-blue flowers in summer	Sun, normal/dry soil. Shear off dead flowerheads after flowering. Clip back in spring
Mahonia japonica	2 x 3m (6 x 10ft)	Fragrant yellow flowers in autumn–spring. Architectural form	Partial shade/shade, moist/normal soil. Prune in mid-spring if necessary
Santolina chamaecyparissus (cotton lavender)	0.5 x 1m (20 x 36in)	Soft, silvery foliage, and yellow button flowers in summer	Sun/partial shade, moist/normal soil. Trim lightly after flowering, and cut back hard in spring
Vinca major **'Variegata'** (periwinkle)	45cm (18in) x indefinite	Glossy, cream-edged foliage, violet-blue flowers spring to autumn. Good groundcover	Sun/partial shade, moist/normal/dry soil (thrives in poor soil). Cut out straggly stems in summer

flowering perennials and annuals

e = evergreen **p** = perennial **h** = hardy annual

Perennials can be cut back after flowering or left until the following spring (see pages 124–5).

	height/spread	special features	care plan
Acanthus spinosus (bear's breeches) **p**	1.5 x 1m (5 x 3ft)	Glossy, spiny foliage and tall spikes of purple and white summer flowers. Architectural	Sun/partial shade/shade, moist/normal soil
Achillea 'Moonshine' (yarrow) **p**	60 x 60cm (2 x 2ft)	Flat heads of yellow flowers from summer to autumn	Sun/partial shade, moist/normal/dry soil
Ajuga reptans 'Burgundy Glow' (bugle) **e p**	0.15 x 1m (6 x 36in)	Purple foliage, and blue flower spikes in spring–summer	Partial shade/shade, moist/normal/dry soil
Alchemilla mollis (lady's mantle) **p**	60 x 75cm (24 x 30in)	Frothy yellow-green flowers in summer, and mounds of pretty grey-green foliage	Sun/partial shade/shade, moist/normal/dry soil. Cut off spent flowerheads
Anthemis punctata subsp. **cupaniana p**	0.30 x 1m (1 x 3ft)	Cushions of silver foliage, and white, daisy-like flowers in summer	Sun, normal/dry soil
Astilbe cvs. p	60–90 x 30–60cm (2–3 x 1–2ft)	Pretty, fern-like foliage, and plumes of red, pink or white summer flowers	Sun/partial shade, moist/normal soil
Astrantia major 'Sunningdale Variegated' (masterwort) **p**	60 x 45cm (24 x 18in)	A mound of bright cream and green foliage, with tall spikes of pink flowers in summer	Sun/partial shade, moist/normal/dry soil
Bergenia cordifolia 'Purpurea' (elephant's ears) **e p**	60 x 75cm (24 x 30in)	Round, red-flushed leaves, and deep pink flowers winter to spring. Good groundcover	Sun/partial shade/shade, moist/normal/dry soil
Brunnera macrophylla p	45 x 60cm (18 x 24in)	Vivid blue flowers in spring. Good groundcover	Partial shade/shade, moist/normal/dry soil
Calendula officinalis (pot marigold) **h**	45 x 30cm (18 x 12in)	Large, orange, daisy-like flowers in summer	Sun, normal/dry soil. Sow seed *in situ* and deadhead regularly
Coreopsis grandiflora (tickseed) **p**	0.45–1 x 0.45m (18–36 x 18in)	Golden-yellow, daisy-like flowers, which are good for cutting, in summer	Sun/partial shade, normal soil
Dicentra spectabilis (bleeding heart) **p**	1 x 0.45m (36 x 18in)	Graceful, ferny foliage, arching stems of pink and white late spring flowers	Sun/partial shade/shade, moist/normal soil
Doronicum orientale (leopard's bane) **p**	60 x 60cm (2 x 2ft)	Bright yellow, daisy-like flowers in spring, earlier than most perennials	Sun/partial shade, normal/dry soil
Erigeron karvinskianus (fleabane) **p**	30 x 60cm (1 x 2ft)	Pink and white, daisy-like summer flowers. Good for walls and crevices	Sun/partial shade, normal/dry soil (thrives in poor soil)
Eschscholzia californica (California poppy) **h**	30 x 30cm (1 x 1ft)	Soft, ferny foliage, and orange, yellow, red, white or pink flowers in summer	Sun, normal/dry soil (thrives in poor soil). Sow seed in situ and deadhead

	height/spread	special features	care plan
Euphorbia polychroma (spurge) **p**	45 x 60cm (18 x 24in)	Acid yellow flowers in late spring to summer.	Sun/partial shade, moist/normal/dry soil
Geranium macrorrhizum **p**	50 x 60cm (20 x 24in)	Cushions of foliage, and pink flowers in summer. Good groundcover	Sun/partial shade/shade, moist/normal/dry soil
Hemerocallis **cvs.** (daylily) **p**	0.45–1 x 0.30–1m (18–36 x 12–36in)	Large yellow, red, pink or orange trumpet flowers and impressive clumps of strap-shaped leaves	Sun/partial shade, moist/normal soil, divide every two to three years
Lamium maculatum 'White Nancy' (deadnettle) **p**	0.15 x 1m (6 x 36in)	Carpet of silvery foliage, spikes of white flowers in summer. Good groundcover	Partial shade/shade, moist/normal/dry soil
Nepeta x faassenii (catmint) **p**	45 x 45cm (18 x 18in)	Mounds of aromatic grey-green leaves and blue-mauve summer flowers	Sun/partial shade, normal/dry soil
Nigella damascena (love-in-a-mist) **h**	45 x 15cm (18 x 6in)	Blue flowers in summer, soft, ferny foliage	Sun, normal/dry soil, sow seed where plants are to flower
Pelargonium **cvs.** (bedding plant) **p**	30–60 x 30–60cm (1–2 x 1–2ft)	Flowers in pink, red or white throughout summer. Tolerates sporadic watering	Sun, normal/dry soil, plant out after risk of frost has passed
Phlox paniculata **p**	1–1.2 x 0.60–1m (3–4 x 2–3ft)	Heads of white, pink or lilac summer flowers, adds height at the back of the border	Sun/partial shade, moist/normal soil
Primula **cvs.** (primrose) **p**	15–25 x 15cm (6–10 x 6in)	Rosette of foliage, flowers in many colours in spring	Sun/partial shade/shade, moist/normal soil
Pulmonaria officinalis (lungwort) **p**	25 x 45cm (10 x 18in)	White- or silver-spotted foliage, sprays of pink and blue flowers in spring	Sun/partial shade/shade, moist/normal/dry soil
Rudbeckia fulgida var. *sullivantii* 'Goldsturm' (coneflower) **p**	60 x 45cm (24 x 18in)	Golden-yellow, daisy-like flowers summer to autumn	Sun/partial shade, moist/normal soil
Saxifraga x urbium (London pride) **e p**	30cm (12in) x indefinite	Rosettes of foliage form a carpet. Stems of frothy pink-white flowers in summer. Good groundcover	Partial shade/shade, moist/normal soil
Sedum spectabile (ice plant) **p**	45 x 45cm (18 x 18in)	Flat heads of pink flowers in late summer and fleshy, grey-green foliage. Attracts bees	Sun/partial shade, normal/dry soil
Solidago **cvs.** (golden rod) **p**	0.60–1.5 x 0.45–0.60m (2–5ft x 18–24in)	Plumes of yellow flowers in late summer and autumn	Sun, normal/dry soil (thrives in poor soil)
Stachys byzantina (lamb's ears) **p**	45 x 60cm (18 x 24in)	A mat of furry, sliver foliage, with spikes of pink-purple flowers in summer	Sun, normal/dry soil
Viola **cvs.** (pansy) (bedding plant) **p**	25 x 25cm (10 x 10in)	Large, showy flowers in many colours, good for shady containers	Sun/partial shade/shade, moist/normal soil

plants for foliage

e = evergreen **p** = perennial **d** = deciduous

	height/spread	special features	care plan
Asplenium scolopendrium (hart's tongue fern) **e**	45 x 60cm (18 x 24in)	Fern, with crowns of straight, solid glossy fronds	Partial shade/shade, moist/normal/dry soil
Briza media (quaking grass) **p**	60 x 30cm (2 x 1ft)	Grass, with long clusters of large grassy heads in summer, makes a pleasant rustling noise in breezy weather	Sun/partial shade, normal/dry soil, cut back dead stems in early spring
Carex elata '**Aurea**' (Bowles' golden sedge) **p**	60 x 45cm (24 x 18in)	Sedge, with arching lime green foliage, fine, grassy seedheads in summer	Sun/partial shade, moist/normal soil, cut back dead stems in early spring
Cortaderia selloana '**Pumila**' (dwarf pampas grass) **e**	1.5 x 1.2m (5 x 4ft)	Grass, with large, fluffy, white or pale pink plumes in late summer, huge clump of arching leaves	Sun, normal/dry soil, cut back dead foliage in spring
Dryopteris filix-mas (male fern) **d**	1 x 1m (3 x 3ft)	Fern, with striking architect ural foliage. The fronds are attractive as they unfurl in spring	Partial shade/shade, moist/normal/dry soil, cut out dead fronds in early spring
Epimedium grandiflorum (barrenwort) **p**	20–30 x 30cm (8–12 x 12in)	White, yellow or pink flowers in spring. The pale green foliage is bronze when young	Partial shade/shade, moist/normal soil, shear off overwintering foliage in spring
Festuca glauca (blue fescue) **e**	30 x 25cm (12 x 10in)	Grass, with clumps of spiky, blue-green foliage, and seed-heads in summer	Sun, normal/dry soil (tolerates poor soil). Trim lightly in spring
Hakonechloa macra '**Aureola**' **p**	45 x 40cm (18 x 16in)	Grass. Arching yellow and green striped leaves, red autumn colour and fine seed-heads late summer to autumn	Sun/partial shade, moist/normal soil. Cut back dead stems in spring
Heuchera micrantha var. *diversifolia* '**Palace Purple**' (coral bells) **e p**	45 x 45cm (18 x 18in)	Clump of metallic purple foliage, fine plumes of pinkish flowers in summer, good for groundcover	Partial shade, moist/normal soil. Divide every two to three years in autumn
Hosta sieboldiana var. *elegans* **p**	60 x 60cm (2 x 2ft)	Large, puckered, blue-green leaves, lilac flowers in summer, the most slug-resistant hosta	Partial shade/shade, moist/normal soil. Cut back dead stems in autumn or spring
Imperata cylindrica '**Rubra**' (Japanese blood grass) **p**	40 x 30cm (16 x 12in)	Grass, green grassy foliage tinted rich blood red, silvery-white grassy seedheads in summer	Sun/partial shade, moist/normal soil. Cut back dead stems in early spring
Miscanthus sinensis '**Zebrinus**' (zebra grass) **p**	1.2 x 1m (4 x 3ft)	Grass, tall clumps of vertical stems, leaves are horizontally banded with gold	Sun/partial shade, moist/normal/dry soil. Cut back in late winter or early spring
Phyllostachys nigra (black bamboo) **e**	3–5 x 2–3m (10–15 x 6–10ft)	Bamboo, with shiny black canes. Architectural	Sun/partial shade, moist/normal soil

	height/spread	special features	care plan
Polypodium vulgare (common polypody) **e**	30 x 30cm (12 x 12in)	Fern, with leathery, ladder-like fronds. Clump-forming	Sun/partial shade/shade, normal/dry soil
Sempervivum cvs. (houseleek) **e p**	8 x 30cm (3 x 12in)	Rosettes of fleshy foliage, and fleshy flower spikes in summer	Sun, normal/dry soil (thrives in poor soil)
Tiarella cordifolia (foam flower) **p**	15–30 x 30cm (6–12 x 12in)	Clumps of handsome foliage, bronze-red autumn colour and plumes of creamy-white flowers in summer	Partial shade/shade, moist/normal soil
Tolmiea menziesii (pick-a-back plant) **p**	0.30–0.60 x 1m (12–24 x 36in)	Clumps of fresh, lime-dappled foliage, and spikes of small green-purple flowers in summer	Partial shade/shade, moist/normal soil

bulbs, tubers and corms   **b** = bulb **c** = cormous **p** = perennial **t** = tuberous

	height/spread	special features	care plan
Allium sphaerocephalon (ornamental onion) **b**	75 x 8cm (30 x 3in)	Round heads of red-purple flowers in summer. It will pop up between other border plants	Sun, normal/dry soil
Anemone blanda (windflower) **p t**	15 x 15cm (6 x 6in)	Blue, pink or white star-like flowers in spring and pretty, ferny foliage. Forms good clumps	Sun/partial shade/shade, normal soil
Crocosmia cvs. (montbretia) **c p**	0.60–1.2 x 0.30–0.60m (2–4 x 1–2ft)	Large clumps of arching, sword-like leaves, and spikes of yellow or orange tubular flowers in summer	Sun/partial shade, moist/normal soil
Crocus cvs. **b**	15 x 5cm (6 x 2in)	Open, vase-like flowers in spring or in autumn	Sun/partial shade, normal/dry soil. Allow foliage to die down naturally
Cyclamen hederifolium **p t**	10 x 15cm (4 x 6in)	Heart-shaped leaves with silver patterns and dainty pink flowers from winter to spring	Partial shade/shade, normal/dry soil
Galanthus nivalis (snowdrop) **b**	10 x 5cm (4 x 2in)	Nodding white flowers in late winter	Partial shade/shade, moist/normal soil
Muscari armeniacum (grape hyacinth) **b**	20 x 15cm (8 x 6in)	Spikes of bright blue flowers in spring	Sun, normal soil. Lift and divide in summer
Narcissus cvs. (daffodil) **b**	30–60 x 10cm (12–24 x 4in)	Bold yellow or white flowers in spring. Many cultivars to choose from	Sun/partial shade, normal/dry soil. Allow leaves to die back naturally
Tulipa cvs. (tulip) **b**	15–60 x 8cm (6–24 x 3in)	Showy flowers in spring in many different colours. Many types are architectural	Sun/partial shade, normal soil. Species and most *greigii* and *kaufmanniana* cvs. can be left in ground; lift others

self-organizer

The following tables feature all the jobs necessary to maintain an easy-care garden

in good shape in just an hour a week. This handy reference will show you what you

should be doing and when you should be doing it, so that you can stay organized and

keep up with jobs to save time later and avert problems. The lists assume that your

garden has been designed with minimal maintenance in mind; if you are making

changes to the garden, you will obviously have to fit in other jobs, such as laying

paving, creating new lawns and covering borders with a weed-suppressing mem-

brane. Although the tables may give the impression that in some weeks there may

be more than an hour's work to do, this is because no garden will contain all of the

features mentioned in the book and so none will require all of the tasks to be done.

spring

surfaces & boundaries   lawns   features

early spring

mow (if dry) ◑

mid-spring

mow and apply feed ◑

mow ◑

mow ◑

late spring

mow ◑

mow ◑   divide pond plants ◔

mow ◑

mow ◑   start to feed fish ◔

◔ = 15 minutes   ◑ = 30 minutes   ◕ = 45 minutes

planting	containers	think ahead	week
cut back dead foliage ◔			1
		buy new shrubs and perennials ◑	2
mulch all bare soil ◑			3
prune late-summer flowering shrubs ◑			4
prune shrubs as the flowers go over ◑			1
plant summer bulbs ◔			2
apply slow-release fertilizer ◔			3
prune shrubs as the flowers go over plant first crop vegetables ◔			4
divide perennials sow hardy annuals in situ ◑			5
prune shrubs as the flowers go over ◔		take garden furniture out of storage ◔	1
weed beds and borders ◔			2
water ◔	plant bedding plants, water ◔		3
prune shrubs as the flowers go over ◔		check barbecue ◔	4

summer

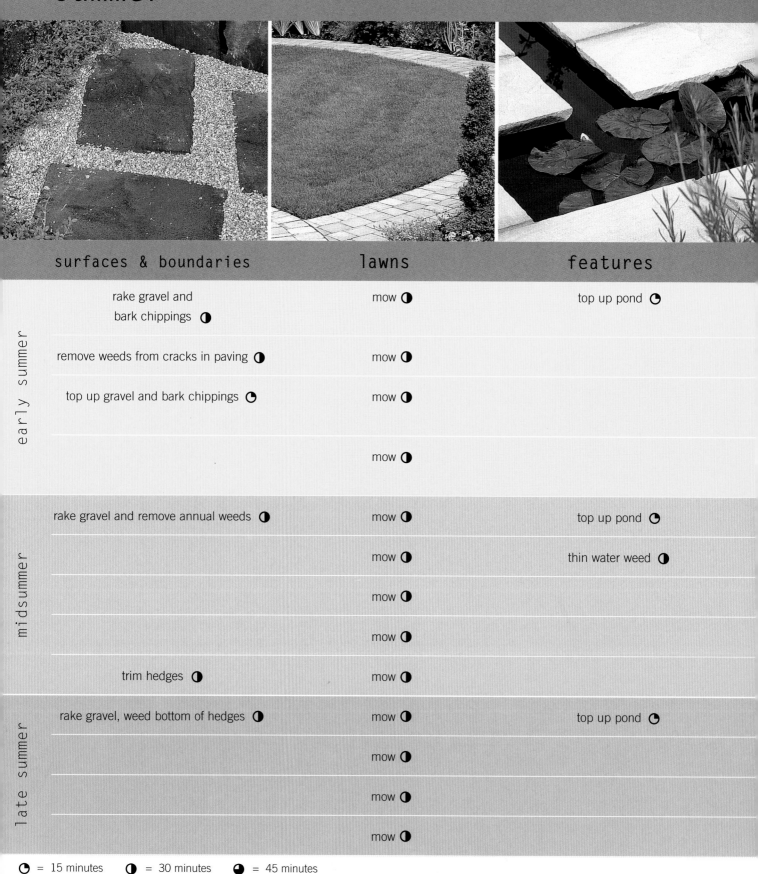

	surfaces & boundaries	lawns	features
early summer	rake gravel and bark chippings ◑	mow ◑	top up pond ◔
	remove weeds from cracks in paving ◑	mow ◑	
	top up gravel and bark chippings ◔	mow ◔	
		mow ◑	
midsummer	rake gravel and remove annual weeds ◑	mow ◔	top up pond ◔
		mow ◔	thin water weed ◑
		mow ◔	
		mow ◔	
	trim hedges ◑	mow ◔	
late summer	rake gravel, weed bottom of hedges ◑	mow ◑	top up pond ◔
		mow ◔	
		mow ◔	
		mow ◔	

◔ = 15 minutes   ◑ = 30 minutes   ◕ = 45 minutes

planting	containers	think ahead	week
water ◕	water ◕		1
water and feed ◕	water and feed ◕		2
water sow second crop vegetables ◑	water ◕		3
prune spring-flowering shrubs, water and feed ◑	water and feed ◕		4
water and deadhead ◕	water and deadhead ◕		1
water, feed and weed ◕	water and feed ◕		2
water ◕	water ◕		3
water and feed ◕	water and feed ◕		4
trim evergreen shrubs ◑	water ◕		5
water, feed and deadhead ◕	water and deadhead ◕		1
water and weed ◕	water ◕		2
water and deadhead ◕	water and deadhead ◕		3
water and weed ◕	water ◕	choose shrubs for autumn planting ◑	4

autumn

surfaces & boundaries	lawns	features

early autumn

	mow ◑	
	mow ◑	
	mow ◑	
	mow ◑	

mid-autumn

	mow ◑	give fish final feed ◔
sweep up fallen leaves ◔		
	mow ◑	clear fallen leaves from pond ◔

late autumn

	mow ◑	
sweep up fallen leaves ◔		clear fallen leaves from pond ◔
	sweep up fallen leaves ◑	

◔ = 15 minutes   ◑ = 30 minutes   ◕ = 45 minutes

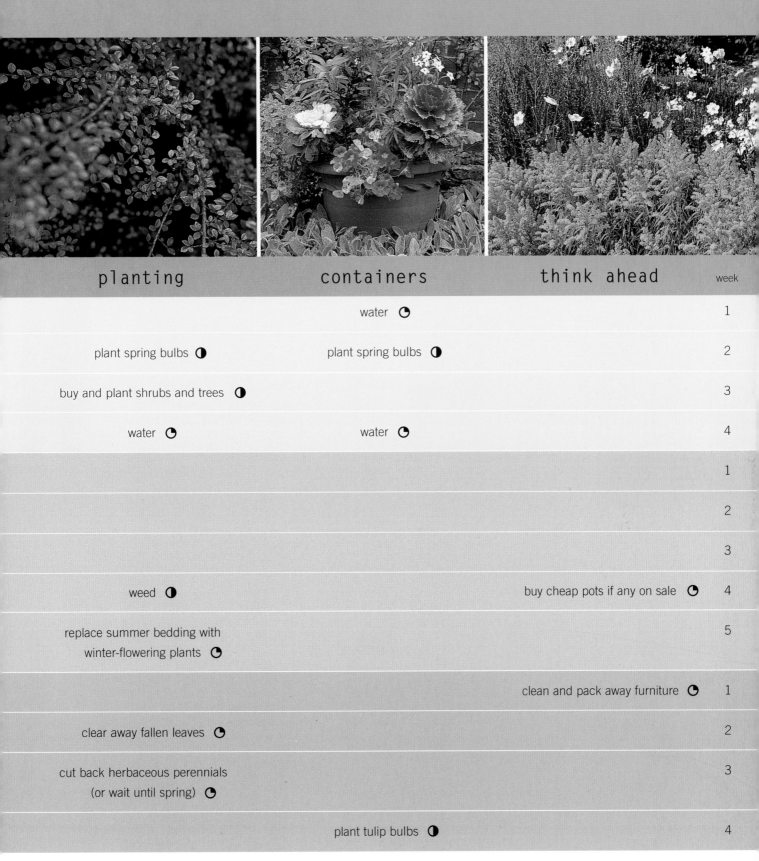

planting	containers	think ahead	week
	water ◐		1
plant spring bulbs ◑	plant spring bulbs ◑		2
buy and plant shrubs and trees ◑			3
water ◐	water ◐		4
			1
			2
			3
weed ◑		buy cheap pots if any on sale ◐	4
replace summer bedding with winter-flowering plants ◐			5
		clean and pack away furniture ◐	1
clear away fallen leaves ◐			2
cut back herbaceous perennials (or wait until spring) ◐			3
	plant tulip bulbs ◑		4

winter

	surfaces & boundaries	lawns	features
early winter			service pond pump ◔
		mow (if dry) ◑	
	sweep up fallen leaves ◔		
mid-winter			stop ice covering pond surface ◔
		have mower serviced ◑	
	repair fences and other structures ◑		
late winter	rake and top up gravel and chippings ◔		
	remove algae and lichen from paths and paving ◑		

◔ = 15 minutes   ◑ = 30 minutes   ◕ = 45 minutes

planting	containers	think ahead	week
			1
cut holly to decorate house ◑		clean pots and tools ◑	2
			3
			4
		buy and plant plants for winter interest ◑	1
			2
plant new trees and shrubs ◐		plan new season's planting ◕	3
		choose hardy annual seeds from catalogue ◕	4
			5
prune winter-flowering shrubs ◕			1
			2
clear away dead leaves and stems ◕			3
prune winter-flowering shrubs ◕			4

ACKNOWLEDGEMENTS
in Source Order

Mark Bolton 46, 65 right, 70, 84 Top /Des; Cannington College, National Amateur Gardening Show 2000 20/Des; First Gardeners, National Amateur Gardening Show 2000 38 **Andrea Jones/Garden Exposures** 6 left, 79 Bottom, 87, 93, 118, 135, 141 right, 154 centre, 155 left/Help the Aged, RHS Chelsea 2000 150 right **Garden Picture Library**/Mark Bolton 94 bottom right/Linda Burgess 103/Erica Craddock 133/Eric Crichton 11 Top, 82/Claire Davies 17 top/Suzie Gibbons 97/John Glover 86/Francoise de Heel 151 right/Marijke Heuff 55/Michael Howes 127/Zara McCalmont 130/ Myer/Le Scanff 69/Clive Nichols 150 left/Michael Paul 112/Jerry Pavia 92/Howard Rice 49, 136, 139/Alec Scaresbrook 131/Friedrich Strauss 134, 138/Ron Sutherland 26 Top, 33 Top, 53,123/Juliette Wade 116 Bottom, 157 right/Mel Watson 51 **John Glover** 26 Bottom, 35, 59/Des; Alan Titchmarsh 14 **Octopus Publishing Group Limited**/Marc Bolton, Des; Elizabeth Apedaile/Garden Design, RHS Hampton Court 2001

152 right/Des; Christopher Colton/Scenic Design Landscaping, RHS Hampton Court 2001 91 right, 129, 152 centre/Des; The Courseworks Design Team/The Mitsubishi Urban Chic Garden, RHS Hampton Court 2000 6 right/Des; Paul Dyer/The Very Interesting Landscape and Water Feature Company, RHS Hampton Court 2001 44, 78/Des; Sally Fell/British Conifer Growers, 'Babylon Garden', RHS Hampton Court 2001 34 Top/Des; Naila Green/Lee Jackson/The Specsaver Optical Group, RHS Hampton Court 2001 96/Des; HMP Leyhill, RHS Chelsea 2001 124/Des; The Marney Hall Consultancy, RHS Hampton Court 2001 153 left/Des; Tony Stuart Smith, The Laurent Perrier Harpers & Queen Garden, RHS Chelsea 2001 31/Des; Brian Tams/Fairscape Design/Chenies Aquatics, RHS Hampton Court 2001 115/des; Xa Tollemache/John Keller, 'The Theatrical Garden', RHS Chelsea 2001 79 top/RHS Hampton Court 2001 80, 152 left, 153 right Andrew Lawson 157 centre/Horward Rice 57 left/David Sarton, Des; David Rosewarne & Maggie Gray, RHS Chelsea 2002/Polly Wreford 102, 110 **Jerry Harpur** 88/Des; Peter

Causer, Roja Dove, Brighton 22 right/Des; Robert Chittock, Seattle, USA 113/Des; Penny Crawhaw 19/Des; Simon Fraser 39/Des; Dr Summer Freeman 43/Des; Stuart Gibbs 32/Des; Arabella Lennox Boyd 30/Des; Jeff Mendoza 27/Jason Payne, Stockwell 60 right/RHS Chelsea '94 50/RHS Chelsea '95 117 **Marcus Harpur** 11 bottom right, 58, 60 left, 75 Bottom, 84 Bottom, 128/An Artist's Garden, RHS Chelsea 01 94 bottom left/Des; Bunny Guinness, RHS Chelsea '97 24/Des; HMP Leyhill, RHS Chelsea 01 100 Top/Pond Farm House, Essex 156 left/Des; Geoff Whiten, RHS Chelsea '01 94 top right **Andrew Lawson** 12, 25, 29, 62, 74, 75 Top, 81, 91 left, 100 Bottom, 155 centre/Brinsbury College, RHS Chelsea 2000 7/Des; Bonita Bulitis/Julia Fogg/Susan Santer, RHS Hampton Court '95 10/Des; Christopher Holliday, Charney Well 15/Des; Prepend Jakobsen 18/Des; David Magson 33 Bottom/Des; Diana May & Mark Watts, RHS Hampton Court 2000 116 Top /Des; Andy Rees 107 Top/Garden in Provence, RHS Chelsea '97 11 bottom left /Des; Simon Shire 34 Bottom/Thomasina Tarling 153 cen-

tre **S & O Mathews** 54 Bottom, 63, 85, 132 **Clive Nichols** 22 left, 48, 54 Top, 66, 73, 89, 111, 141 left/Richard Coward 154 right/Des; Lucy Huntington, RHS Chelsea '94 41/Des; Claire Mathews/Avant Gardener 65 left, 114/Des; Andrew & Karla Newell 71/Jane Nichols 98/The Nichols Garden, Reading 57 right/The Old Vicarage, Norfolk 148, 156 centre/Des; R & J Passmore 106/RHS Chelsea '98 17 Bottom, 21/Des; Woking Borough Council, RHS Chelsea '93 67/Des; Steven Woodhams, RHS Chelsea '97 151 centre **Harry Smith Collection** 83, 108, 109, 119, 125, 126, 130, 140, 150 centre, 151 left, 154 left, 155 right, 156 right, 157 left **Juliette Wade**//Des; Joy & Jerry Eveley 107 Bottom Des; Brian Wigley 13

Executive Editor: Emily van Eesteren
Project Editor: Sarah Ford
Copy-editors: Lydia Darbyshire and Cathy Lowne
Indexer: Hilary Bird
Senior Designer: Rozelle Bentheim
Book Designer: Geoff Borin
Picture Researcher: Claire Gouldstone
Production Controller: Jo Sim